SMART from the START

JAMES H. STRONGE | JESSICA M. STRAESSLE | XIANXUAN XU

SMART
from the
START

100 Tools for Teaching with Confidence

ascd
Arlington, Virginia USA

2800 Shirlington Road, Suite 1001 • Arlington, VA 22206 USA
Phone: 800-933-2723 or 703-578-9600 • Fax: 703-575-5400
Website: www.ascd.org • Email: member@ascd.org
Author guidelines: www.ascd.org/write

Richard Culatta, *Chief Executive Officer*; Anthony Rebora, *Chief Content Officer*; Genny Ostertag, *Managing Director, Book Acquisitions & Editing*; Mary Beth Nielsen, *Director, Book Editing*; Megan Doyle, *Editor*; Thomas Lytle, *Creative Director*; Donald Ely, *Art Director*; Georgia Park, *Senior Graphic Designer*; Melissa Johnston/The Hatcher Group, *Graphic Designer*; Valerie Younkin, *Senior Production Designer*; Kelly Marshall, *Production Manager*; Shajuan Martin, *E-Publishing Specialist*; Christopher Logan, *Senior Production Specialist*

PAPERBACK ISBN: 978-1-4166-3194-1   ASCD product #122009 n7/23

PDF E-BOOK ISBN: 978-1-4166-3195-8; see Books in Print for other formats.

Quantity discounts are available: email programteam@ascd.org or call 800-933-2723, ext. 5773, or 703-575-5773. For desk copies, go to www.ascd.org/deskcopy.

Library of Congress Cataloging-in-Publication Data
Names: Stronge, James H., author. | Straessle, Jessica M., author. | Xu, Xianxuan, author.
Title: Smart from the start : 100 tools for teaching with confidence / James H. Stronge, Jessica M. Straessle, Xianxuan Xu.
Other titles: One hundred fifty tools for teaching with confidence
Description: Arlington, Virginia USA : ASCD, [2023] | Includes bibliographical references and index.
Identifiers: LCCN 2023003077 (print) | LCCN 2023003078 (ebook) | ISBN 9781416631941 (paperback) | ISBN 9781416631958 (pdf)
Subjects: LCSH: First year teachers. | Teacher effectiveness. | Classroom management. | Teaching—Aids and devices.
Classification: LCC LB2844.1.N4 S785 2023 (print) | LCC LB2844.1.N4 (ebook) | DDC 371.102—dc23/eng/20230301
LC record available at https://lccn.loc.gov/2023003077
LC ebook record available at https://lccn.loc.gov/2023003078

31 30 29 28 27 26 25 24 23   1 2 3 4 5 6 7 8 9 10 11 12

SMART from the START | 100 Tools for Teaching with Confidence

Part 4: Delivering Quality Instruction and Engaging Students in Learning

Part 5: Assessment of and for Learning

Part 6: Finding Yourself in the Classroom

Introduction

Developing any book starts with imagination—imagination about a topic where we might be able to connect with readers and, hopefully, contribute to the readers' growth and learning. What sparked our imagination to even contemplate *Smart from the Start: 100 Tools for Teaching with Confidence* was new teachers themselves. The experiences of new teachers are unique and important, and you learn so much in your first few years that will affect you for the rest of your career. In your preparation to be a teacher, you may have longed to have a class of your own, and now is your opportunity! We sincerely hope the book serves to help you be the most successful teacher possible.

Vignette 1

I remember so well what it was like to be a new 7th grade social studies teacher in my first teaching assignment. I had just completed my undergraduate degree with a major in history and a minor in English. Additionally, I had the benefit of a teacher preparation program, including a rewarding student teaching experience guided by a wonderful cooperating teacher as my mentor. Nonetheless, when I arrived at my new school on the very first day, I realized pretty quickly I was in big trouble. My homeroom—and two of my teaching assignments each day—was a class of all 7th grade girls. And let me say, nothing, absolutely nothing, in my training to be a history teacher prepared me for the world of 7th grade girls! I learned very quickly that until I could understand pre-adolescent psychology and, specifically, the interests and lives of these 7th graders, I would never ever be any good at teaching history. As the year progressed, I learned so much from my students. They taught me that you don't teach subjects, and you don't teach classes; you teach students—one at time. And they taught me that when I learned to care deeply for my students, and to demonstrate that caring in tangible, relevant ways, then and only then, could I even begin to understand what it means to be a teacher.

While I learned tremendously from my students and quickly learned to appreciate them and enjoyed coming to school each day, I'm not so sure the learning for my students was reciprocal. They struggled because I struggled, and they often had to suffer through my efforts of learning how to teach. This experience has always remained vivid in my memory. And while I know that so many novice teachers are far better prepared to enter their first classroom and positively guide their students, it still reminds me that there is a steep learning curve that all new teachers experience. It is for these teachers in their first few years of teaching that this book is intended.

James H. Stronge

Vignette 2

I remember the first class I ever taught and the impact the students had on my career. They challenged me to meet their individual needs and search for better ways to ensure each child had the opportunity to learn and grow in a manner that was consistent with who they were as individuals. With the guidance and help of my principal and fellow teachers, I was able to have a wonderful and fruitful year with my class. Those relationships among the adults in the building, as well as the relationships I built with my students, were key in my experience. My hope is that this book will help you prepare for the early stages of your teaching career by giving you tools to become the best and most effective teacher you can be as you focus on the many individual needs of the students in your care.

Jessica M. Straessle

Vignette 3

The first year of teaching is like a roller coaster ride—it can be intimidating and exhilarating at the same time. For all who have ever taught, we know that this first year can be extraordinarily challenging. When the rubber meets the road, beginning teachers are confronted with the reality of the classroom and encounter unexpected situations, many of which simply couldn't be addressed in their teacher preparation programs.

The good news is that quality mentoring and induction hold great potential to positively impact the quality and retention of new teachers. Actually, gains in teacher effectiveness associated with experience are most dramatic in a teacher's initial years, so the first few years of teaching are the prime time to hone and polish a teacher's practice. We know that new teachers need structured support; they simply can't be left to "sink or swim" in the critical early years of teaching. It's my hope that the book can help serve as a practical guide for beginning teachers that will help ease the transition into a sustainable and rewarding teaching career.

Xianxuan Xu

Conceptual Framework for the Book

The framework for *Smart from the Start: 100 Tools for Teaching with Confidence* is provided in Figure 1, which outlines five key qualities for understanding and prioritizing the teacher's work. These qualities, based on a thorough literature review on teaching effectiveness, capture well the essence of the teacher's work.

Each quality serves as the basis of discussion for the six parts included in the book. The book is composed of a total of 30 mini-chapters, each light in text, but heavy with practical tools (e.g., forms, checklists, templates) that new teachers can immediately apply in their practice. Each chapter focuses on one specific strategy or practice and is only a few pages long. The chapters each include a brief summary of the latest research related to the topic, followed with practical tips and techniques on how to put the ideas into practice. We designed the materials in a manner that teachers can copy, apply, or adapt for immediate use. Additionally, the style and format are intended to be user-friendly, thus, providing an easy-to-use "workbook" for teachers to apply throughout their first few years in the classroom and beyond.

Smart from the Start: 100 Tools for Teaching with Confidence relies heavily on the most current research to build a clear pathway to effective teaching practices. Throughout our work on the book, the predominant filter for considering a chapter topic was pretty simple: What do new teachers need to know and be able to do if they are to survive and, then, thrive? The framework that we ultimately settled on is represented in the following figure.

The research findings and recommended practices identified in *Smart from the Start: 100 Tools for Teaching with Confidence* will be familiar to experienced teachers and, hopefully, recognized by our new teacher colleagues. New teachers, we trust the book serves as a resource that you can keep nearby and draw from as you need to enhance your understanding and to use the tools in your teaching.

Uses for the Book

By identifying and carefully considering the attributes that especially relate to new teachers, we hope to be better equipped to identify links between novice teacher practices and desirable student outcomes. Thus, *Smart from the Start: 100 Tools for Teaching with Confidence,* is aimed at improving the quality of new teacher practices. In this effort, the book can be a valuable resource for the following audiences:

- Novice teachers, first and foremost, this book is for you. By novice teachers, we especially are considering teachers in their first three years or so of teaching.

- Administrators who supervise and support novice teachers, we hope the book can offer you guidance to help your novice teachers improve their practices in real and practical ways.

- Instructional coaches, as you work to support your novice teachers to acclimate, grow, and flourish in their new positions, we think the tools included in each chapter may be especially helpful to provide tangible support.

FIGURE I.1 Framework for Support and Success

Part 1: Getting Ready for the Start of School	Part 1 looks at the basics of getting ready for the school year from getting settled in the school to preparing those first lesson plans and what to do on the first day. This part will help you feel connected to your school, confident in your preparation, and prepared for your students and their families.
Part 2: Classroom Management and the Learning Environment	Part 2 gets down to the nitty gritty of classroom management and establishing a learning environment conducive to optimal learning. These chapters will give you the knowledge and skill needed to bring about a positive school experience for all.
Part 3: Instructional Planning	Part 3 examines lesson planning, ensuring the needs of all students are met, and suggests ways to plan collaboratively.
Part 4: Instruction and Engaging Students in Learning	Part 4 explores different ways to teach students that keeps them motivated and engaged. This section will help you branch out and consider various ways to teach different topics.
Part 5: Assessment of and for Learning	Part 5 considers how and why we assess students. From ensuring alignment to informing instruction to focusing on different assessment possibilities, this part will help you understand why assessment is vital in understanding what students know but also what they need to learn next!

For any user of the book, we hope our writing is abundantly clear that there are only two things, beyond safety, that really matter in schools—and they are 1) supporting effective teaching, and 2) helping students be the best they can be. Our job is to change children's lives for the better—in one classroom at a time and for one student at a time. It is to these ends that we hope you find *Smart from the Start: 100 Tools for Teaching with Confidence* valuable.

PART 1

Getting Ready for the Start of School

CHAPTERS 1–8

Prepare to start your school year in an organized and thoughtful manner to promote student achievement and growth as you work with families to meet students' needs.

1 Familiarizing Yourself with the New Working Environment

The New Kid in School

Being the new kid in school is never easy. You need to learn the climate and culture of the school as well as fall into step with routines, coworkers, students, parents, and administration. Just as every classroom has a teacher with their own style, each school will have its own style and way of doing things, and it's important to blend the teacher's personal style for running the classroom with the expectations and routines of the school. In fact, research shows that one of the most challenging aspects of being a new teacher is adjusting to workplace routines (Dimitroff & Dimitroff, 2018). The high workload and stress that accompany the job add to the difficulty of this adjustment, and, depending on the type of school setting, this challenge can vary (Chaaban & Du, 2017; Gaikhorst et al., 2017).

Adjusting to a New Workplace

Many schools and districts may offer teacher induction programs prior to the beginning of the school year. These programs help teachers better assimilate into their new work setting in order to improve their satisfaction and success and decrease attrition (Ronfeldt & McQueen, 2017). If you are involved in an induction program, look at it as an opportunity. Key points of most new teacher induction programs relate to establishing an orientation program and selecting a mentor teacher (Kearney, 2017). The orientation program can be at the school level, the district level, or both levels. This will help you acclimate to the climate and culture of the school and district. Additionally, it will get you started in figuring out the routines of the workplace as well as give you a support person—a mentor teacher—to support your continued induction and professional growth.

When trying to adjust to a new situation, it is always important to know how your predecessors accomplished this feat. Advice from newer teachers can be beneficial and help you gain your footing. While it can feel like a lot of a teacher's work can be non-teaching, including time-intensive preparation, remember that teachers gain a lot of personal satisfaction that the work they do makes a difference (Chaaban & Du, 2017). In fact, there are many ways you can adjust to your new workplace and feel satisfied in your job. Figure 1.1 presents advice from novice teachers about ways to help you adjust and lead a more satisfying work environment.

FIGURE 1.1: Novice Teachers' Advice to Others

Personal Satisfaction	Interpersonal Satisfaction	Organizational Satisfaction
• Learn about yourself and the new culture around you. • Rely on your training to become a teacher. • Build an encouraging and supportive environment. • Enjoy your students and know you are making a difference.	• Find a go-to person. • Ask for help when needed. • Develop good relationships with coworkers.	• Work with your administration to address the new teacher workload. • Find ways to work with your administration to ensure you feel comfortable as the leader in your own classroom.

Source: Information from Chaaban & Du (2017) and Dimitroff & Dimitroff (2018).

🔧 Tools to Use

TOOL 1.1: Go-to List

A challenge for new teachers is getting used to the workplace routines. Part of these routines is knowing who to go to for help. Within the school there are various staff members who have specialized jobs, and, as a new teacher, you will most likely work with each person for myriad reasons. This form can help you to organize your go-to people. Knowing the contact person and how to work with them will help you assimilate into the pace of the workplace.

Attendance	
Behavior	
Child Study	
ESL/ELL	
Gifted/Talented	
Guidance	
Mentor Teacher	
Special Needs Teachers	
Team Lead	
Technology Issues	

TOOL 1.2: Questions to Ask

Talk to any teacher and they will tell you that asking questions is an essential aspect for helping a novice teacher "learn the ropes" at a new school. There are a lot of policies and procedures when adjusting to a new work environment, and, while teacher induction may address many of these questions, each school or workplace will have its own practices and preferences for "the way we do things around here." If you know (or can quickly learn) the answers to these practical, day-to-day questions, it will help you feel less stress and give you a pulse on the routines for your school. In addition, asking these questions of your mentor or colleagues will help you build a support system within your workspace.

Familiarizing Yourself with Your Workplace: Find the Answers for These Questions:

- ☐ How do I set up my email account?
- ☐ How do I set up my voicemail (if you have a phone in your classroom)?
- ☐ How do I arrange for a substitute?
- ☐ What do standard substitute plans look like in this building?
- ☐ Who do I call if there is an emergency and I am unable to come into work or if there is an emergency on the way to work?
- ☐ Where is the teacher workroom?
- ☐ When do I need to lock my classroom?

☐ How do I help keep the classroom secure throughout the day?

☐ How do I report a disciplinary problem?

☐ What do I do if I have to use the bathroom in the middle of the day?

☐ What is the procedure for setting up field trips?

☐ Where can I secure regular and supplemental texts?

☐ What is the procedure if I must collect money from students?

☐ What are the arrival and dismissal procedures?

☐ What are the procedures and expectations for classes, teachers, and students in the common areas (e.g., lunchroom, hallways, bathrooms, water fountains, atrium)?

☐ Where can I find a janitor if I need one?

☐ What are the rules for food in the classrooms or hallways?

☐ Is there a dress code for teachers, and what are the expectations for professional dress?

☐ When are back-to-school events?

☐ When are parent/guardian conferences?

☐ What is the general practice for setting up parent/guardian conferences?

☐ When are staff meetings/grade level meetings/content area group meetings?

☐ What technology is available?

☐ How many grades are expected per class each grading period?

☐ Am I able to get back into the building after school hours if I forgot something? How?

☐ What is the homework policy?

☐ Can I use outside materials for my lessons, or do I need to stick with only curriculum materials?

☐ How do you work with the PTA?

☐ Is there a schoolwide policy on parent volunteers?

☐ How do most teachers arrange for parent volunteers to help?

Source: Adapted from Baker (n.d.) and NCAE 2020.

2 Arranging the Classroom and Getting Organized

The Ins and Outs of Classroom Arrangement and Organization

Before the school year starts, setting aside a few days to get your classroom ready can pay dividends in the long run. Having a well-organized classroom in advance of school opening will help you have a sense of readiness. Also, by being well-organized and prepared, you portray composure and confidence when students and their parents first walk through the classroom door. You get one shot at this opportunity and, if you fumble, they will recognize any disorganization and unpreparedness.

By being ready when the first school day starts, you will be able to convey the clear message that you are ready to teach and the students will be ready to learn. Further, your early preparation serves the goal of creating an inviting classroom environment that is conducive to learning. This preliminary work should include developing functional floor plans (considering both teacher and student work areas), wall spaces, and supplies. In a very practical sense, something as simple as the way you arrange and organize the room and materials will affect how you will interact with your students and how the students will engage with learning (Hamilton, 2019). Investing early in your classroom and being prepared, well-planned, and organized directly contributes to increased student learning by freeing up more time on actual learning and reducing time on noninstructional activities (McLean et al., 2016).

Organization is important for creating and sustaining a quality classroom learning environment. In a practical sense, organizing is mostly a matter of planning and thinking through what you want to accomplish and how you go about accomplishing the work. Remember: good organization = good learning! We have included a number of checklists and tips that may help you get started with making your classroom ready for students.

🔧 Tools to Use

TOOL 2.1: Getting Ready Checklist

This tool will help you get your classroom organized for the beginning of the school year. After preparing your classroom, walk around *as if you were a student* and ensure that the room works for both you and your students.

- ☐ I have arranged classroom furniture to define learning areas.
- ☐ I have secured a sufficient amount of student desks, tables, and chairs, and I have created seating charts.
- ☐ The arrangement of the classroom shows a clearly defined traffic pattern to ease transitions during the learning.
- ☐ I have arranged my own work area where I have binders and folders appropriately labeled to contain assignments, rubrics, quizzes, tests, handouts, lecture notes, and more.
- ☐ I have set up the grade book (physical or electronic), which has a list of students' names, the categories of activities/assignments/quizzes/tests, and the way they will be recorded and aggregated.
- ☐ I have set up physical file folders or electronic folders that will be used to organize and manage each student's information and designated a section in the folders to record communication with parents and families.
- ☐ I have set up the bookshelves and, where appropriate, provided a low-maintenance checkout process and attached a printed sign-out sheet to the shelf for students to easily record when they check out or return books or materials.
- ☐ I have maximized the accessibility and availability of learning materials.
- ☐ I know how I will communicate to students about the organization of space and, where necessary, materials are to be stored.
- ☐ I have created an inviting space by decorating the bulletin boards and walls.
- ☐ I have secured all the necessary supplies and have a list of items that I can refer to regularly for quick restocking.
- ☐ I have tested the technology in the classroom to make sure everything is operating appropriately.
- ☐ I have checked the safety of the classroom to make sure windows, shelves, electrical outlets, and everything else are in good working condition.

TOOL 2.2: A Few Tips for Quick Organization

Being comfortable in your space is important. If you are comfortable, then your students will feel more comfortable. These tips will help you feel organized and make your classroom feel like home.

- The layout of the classroom should work for your pedagogical style as well as the preferred learning environment according to students' ages. Remember, a key goal is to maximize student engagement, and classroom layout matters.

- Assigning each student with a number may help save time in organization. These numbers can be used to line students up, check quickly who missed homework (students will be asked to put their number on the upper right corner of their work), and organize cubbies.

- Get to know your custodian personally, show your appreciation, and seek help politely. The custodian plays an important role helping you maintain a clean and well-organized classroom every day.

- Place commonly used materials such as scissors, staplers, tape, and glues in easily accessible places for students so you won't need to be the sole distributor of such resources.

- Your classroom library can be a valuable and important resource, especially if your school doesn't have a well-established library for your subject area. To prepare for your in-class library, collaborate with your community or school librarians to locate books that appeal to your students and match with their reading levels. Consider organizing the books by genres (e.g., classic, graphic fiction, science fiction, historical fiction, poetry, dystopia, mystery, memoir, and nonfiction). Also, consider using the top shelves for a display of related and interesting themes such as "holiday reads," "books made into movies," or subject matters that students will be learning.

- Library Thing (www.librarything.com) is a free website that allows you to have an easy library-quality catalog for your classroom books. You type in the book's title or author, and the website will search sources such as Amazon.com or the Library of Congress to locate the photo of a specific book cover and facts about the book. You also can customize your tags and notes to the books. And do not forget to stick a label or put a stamp on the books to indicate they belong to your class; in case any end up in the school's lost and found, they can be returned to you.

TOOL 2.3: Checklist of School Supplies

This list can help you get started with supplies you will need for the school year. While most schools have school supply lists for students, it is important to remember that not all students will arrive with the supplies they need, so you need to have supplies ahead of time.

- ☐ White paper and color paper
- ☐ Printer and cartridges
- ☐ Glue sticks
- ☐ Stapler and staples
- ☐ Staple remover
- ☐ Whiteouts or correction tape
- ☐ Labels
- ☐ Dry-erase markers
- ☐ Marker board eraser
- ☐ Caddies
- ☐ Highlighters
- ☐ Tape
- ☐ Hole punch
- ☐ Binder clips
- ☐ Paper clips
- ☐ Pencils and pens
- ☐ Pencil sharpener
- ☐ Erasers
- ☐ Hand sanitizer
- ☐ Clock
- ☐ Paper towel
- ☐ Tissues
- ☐ Folders
- ☐ Binders
- ☐ Rubber bands
- ☐ Clipboards
- ☐ Trash can
- ☐ Recycle bin
- ☐ Baskets
- ☐ Sticky notes
- ☐ Index cards
- ☐ Calendar (or monthly or weekly planner)
- ☐ Scissors
- ☐ Notebooks

1

TOOL 2.4: What Works and What Doesn't Work in Classroom Decorations

Using decorations to put your personal touch on your classroom is important and gives you a way to make the classroom inviting to students. When choosing decorations, remember that less is more. Heavily decorated classrooms with too much visual stimulus actually can compromise students' cognitive performance (such as focus, memory, self-regulation, ability to concentrate) according to a number of research studies (Barrett et al., 2015; Barrett et al., 2017; Rodrigues & Pandeirada, 2018). So, be selective in the decorations you use and how much you use throughout the classroom; aim for attractive and inviting but avoid distracting decor.

What Works	What Does Not Work
• Keep naturalness in the classroom, such as natural light, good air quality, and links to nature. • Allow for flexibility so the classroom and wall areas have a variety of learning activities and reflect new material and regular changes. • Use photos or displays of inclusive role models and inspirational quotes to build connections with students. • Display student work to encourage student ownership of the classroom. • Hang posters (e.g., maps, diagrams) that can reinforce learning, and change them regularly to only use visual aids that can assist student learning that is germane at the given point in time. • Keep 20–50 percent of the wall area clear of decorations. • Selectively use bold colors in certain areas but keep the rest in muted colors.	• Don't overuse visually complex decorations. • Avoid clutter and chaos. • Be mindful of posters and quotes where students' cultural backgrounds and interests are not represented. • Do not display materials that distract students rather than boost their learning.

TOOL 2.5: Tips for Organizing Information

The most time-consuming part of classroom organization may have to do with recording and organizing information related to teaching and learning.

Anecdotal Note-Keeping	Set up a template for daily or weekly anecdotal notes and make copies (if you prefer paper copy) so you can use them throughout the year. The template can be as simple as a table where each cell has a student's name. The purpose of this document (electronic or physical) is to take quick, frequent, and formative notes about each individual student's academic and behavioral performance. You also can use the document to record your observations, the interventions you use for each student, or the contacts you make with the parents. Over time, those anecdotal notes will give you a quick longitudinal overview of the whole class's performance.
Individual Learner Records	Set up physical files or electronic folders for each student to organize and manage student information. These files can serve as the learner profile, where you can keep student work, assessment data, and reflections on students' strengths and weaknesses of learning. These files can be shared with students for their input and reflections. Also, these files should be living documents that reflect how each individual student develops and grows in the learning process. If it works for you, you can also include some of the relevant anecdotal notes regarding a particular student as part of their learner profile.
Teaching Materials Cabinet	Have a file cabinet designated for your teaching materials. Depending on your preference, you may consider having about 25 folders in the cabinet, with each folder labeled for each of the school days of the month. This approach can help you plan a month's teaching in advance. At the beginning of each day or ahead of the day, you can just grab the appropriate folder and know what to cover and deliver that day. The folder can hold worksheets, exit tickets, handouts, and homework. Of course, this approach can work on a weekly basis as well.

Alternatively, you can also organize your file cabinet of teaching materials by units, learning goals, or learning standards. Also, don't forget to have a folder with lessons for your substitute teacher. Do this now; you can't always predict when you will be absent. |

 Words to Know

Anecdotal notes—notes taken by the teacher to document what happened in the classroom

Individual learner record—a collection of student information and student work

Classroom Rules and Student Behavior

Classroom Rules Matter

One of the areas of teaching that novice teachers tend to find most daunting is classroom management. Your class more or less functions like an organization, and for any robust and smooth-running organization there should be sound policies and guidelines. Your students will expect and respect behavioral boundaries that are fairly established and implemented. Additionally, any classroom without rules and behavioral expectations is susceptible to off-task behaviors, disruptions, and aggressions that will take learning time away from every student in the class.

One of the key characteristics of effective teachers is that they hold and clearly communicate academic and behavioral expectations to students (Gottfried & Ansari, 2019). Unfortunately, student discipline plays an important role in affecting a teacher's job satisfaction and burnout (García-Carmona et al., 2019; Malinen & Savolainen, 2016). Therefore, it is very important to establish clear behavioral expectations and patterns with the students at the beginning of a school year. Your students will actually welcome reasonable and fair discipline, and they will be happier and more satisfied, just like you are, in a safe, orderly, and well-functioning classroom environment.

This down payment of effort at the beginning of the school year will pay dividends throughout the year by protecting instructional time and preventing learning time from being lost to disruptions or distractions that are preventable. Think of this simple calculation:

> What if you could save a mere five minutes of instructional time each class period each day by simply having a few classroom guidelines in place that help you be better organized and keep your students on task? Those five minutes a day per class period would equal 25 minutes a week (almost a half-hour)! And if we multiply the five minutes a day by a conservative 180 days for an academic year, that equals 900 minutes—or 15 hours of instructional time.

So, we get almost three more instructional days per academic year, and this figure is only an estimate for a class period. What if you save even more time for a full day if you teach in a self-contained classroom? While it seems like a little thing, having a few well-functioning classroom rules and procedures turns out to be a big deal: It's the gift that keeps on giving!

Getting Student Buy-in for Classroom Rules

It is important to ensure you have classroom rules that are clearly articulated and set expectations for students; however, the teacher is only part of the classroom. The students need to own the rules, as well, for a robust learning environment and for order to be maintained. So how do you get students to buy into the rules? First and foremost, begin on day one by building relationships with your students. Knowing your students and letting them get to know you goes a long way in establishing trust and understanding. By understanding who they are as individuals, you can learn about their motives to either follow or not follow the rules. Additionally, by recognizing the individuality of students and using proactive behavior management strategies, students can recognize that the rules allow them to grow and learn as individuals in a harmonious environment (Aelterman et al., 2019).

Words to Know

***Student buy-in*—** a process used to help students feel a sense of belonging and ownership of the learning environment

In the following tools you can see an example of how to individualize the rules. This approach tends to work well with students in 4th grade and up, but for younger students, you may need to take additional steps. In addition to building relationships with students, tying rules to positive consequences and teaching students the rules in an explicit manner have been found to be effective in getting younger student buy-in (Alter & Haydon, 2017). Teaching students the rules in an explicit manner helps them understand what is expected and why, which helps garner student buy-in. While most teachers carefully review and discuss classroom rules and state them clearly, teaching the rules takes time and finesse. That time will be worth it, however, as student ownership of the rules will create a symbiotic atmosphere where teaching and learning are the responsibility of both the teacher and students. And the result will be a more robust and productive classroom learning environment.

⚒ Tools to Use

TOOL 3.1: Attributes of Effective Classroom Policies and Guidelines

These tips will help as you begin thinking about what you want your classroom policies and procedures to be in your classroom.

1. Be clear and positive when delineating rules.
2. It's better to have a few good rules that you implement than a host of rules to which you only pay lip service. Don't have rules that you can't consistently implement.
3. Be fair and consistent when enforcing rules. All rules apply to everyone.
4. Respect diversity and make the classroom inclusive.
5. Create rules and guidelines that are fair as a key aspect of the classroom climate.

TOOL 3.2: Things to Consider When Making Classroom Rules

Your classroom rules and their enforcement will help make your classroom a safe space where all students know the expectations and where all can learn. While creating rules may seem easy, ensuring the rules work for you and the students can be challenging. This list offers some things to consider before creating and implementing classroom rules.

First of all, consult your district's code of conduct to gain an understanding about school guidelines for discipline procedures. Regardless, you *must* be consistent.

- What are the homework policies?

- What happens for missed or late assignments?

- Will you use point deduction for all assignments that are late?

- Will you allow flexible deadlines or give full credit for late work?

- Will you investigate and understand why an assignment is late (e.g., student behavioral problem; lack of time, space, technology, and resources at home; the assignment being too challenging)?

- Will you penalize students by not providing feedback or a redo opportunity for a late assignment?

- Or will you keep a work habits grade that is separate from students' performance on subject content mastery? (If allowed by your school policy, this is recommended.)

What are students' expectations for interactions with peers? Ask questions such as "How do I want the students to treat each other?"

- Focus on positive discipline. What are the rewards for following classroom rules?

- Will you give extra credit for desired behaviors?

- What will be the options for recognitions (e.g., allowing the student to pick a game at recess, be the teacher's helper for a day, choose any class job for a day or week)?

- And even better, can you simply eliminate the extrinsic rewards once students readily adopt the classroom rules as their own?

When positive discipline doesn't work, what are the consequences for breaking a classroom rule? The consequences can take a progressive form such as a warning, losing a privilege, isolation from a group, parent notification, and referral to the principal. Progression can work, but keep it simple.

What kind of behavior justifies a discipline referral? Exclusionary discipline, such as suspension (whether in-school or out-of-school) or, for the most extreme problems, expulsion, is the last resort for discipline strategies because they remove students from learning and can result in further school disengagement. Minor misconducts or willful defiance, such as smaller classroom disruptions, less severe but inappropriate verbal language, failure to follow procedures, and use of electronic devices for noneducational purposes do not have to be punished by suspension. These behaviors often can be improved through pro-social approaches. However, exclusionary discipline must be in place when student violence, extreme harassment, or possession of alcohol, drugs, or a weapon—more severe forms of student misconduct—is involved to ensure other students' safety and learning. Always remember that safety is ultimately most important; teaching and learning is everything else!

TOOL 3.3: Sample Behavioral Expectation Statements

Creating classroom rules from scratch can be a daunting task. To assist with this important responsibility, this checklist provides some possible behavioral expectations you might want to include for students. Consider turning these expectations into classroom promises using "we" statements. Also, talking with other grade-level teachers and your mentor can help you refine the list for your teaching assignment and location.

> Treat others the way you want to be treated and treat your classmates with respect and kindness.

> Treat the teacher with respect and kindness.

> Actions that disrupt the learning process are not acceptable.

> Respect others' personal belongings.

> Respect others' personal space, rights, and property.

> Follow directions for all learning activities.

> Actively participate in every lesson every day.

> Complete your assignments and tasks on time.

> Keep the classroom neat and orderly.

> Come to class prepared to learn from the beginning to the end of the class period.

> Raise your hand and wait to be called on before you speak.

> Listen quietly while others are speaking.

> Be responsible for your own learning.

> Keep your hands to yourself.

> Stay in your seat except when there is a good reason to move around.

> Clean up after yourself and help maintain a clean classroom.

> Use quiet voices in the classroom and hallways.

> Always do your best.

TOOL 3.4: Should You Be a Friend or an Authority Figure?

As a new teacher, you may feel conflicted about whether you should form relationships or friendships with the students, or whether assuming the role of an authority figure should take precedent. The answer is that both matter. You may already have heard of the expression "warm demander," which is often used to describe effective teachers who extend warmth and invite students into their own learning but, at the same time, are persistent in exerting discipline and expecting the best from the students. The combination of warmth and demand is positively related to student behavior and learning (McLean et al., 2020). Thus, striking this balance is vital.

Building Relationships	Assuming Authority
• Get to know your students as individuals and build rapport.	• Establish a disciplined and structured learning environment.
• Have fun with students appropriately within the classroom.	• Mean what you say and follow what you say with actions.
• Share hilarious, harmless jokes to laugh with students.	• Use positive, but assertive body language when giving directions.
• Build trust.	• Be clear, consistent, and fair when implementing rules.
• Show that you truly care.	• Use the firm, calm "teacher voice."
• Be pleasant and positive (avoid using intimidation to coerce students to behave).	• Stand tall and pull your shoulders back to show confidence.
• Communicate respect.	• Make eye contact with students.
• Share appropriate personal stories to be personable.	• Demand that students demonstrate self-discipline, not just compliance.

TOOL 3.5: Using Contracts for Student Buy-in

Using a student commitment contract helps to get buy-in from students by giving them the ability to individualize their needs for the classroom. While it will still be necessary for the teacher to develop classroom rules from the themes of what students provide, this tool allows the students to think deeply about who they are as individuals, their learning, and learning needs, and to make commitments to the whole class. It also gives students an idea of what they can expect from the teacher. As written, this is for older students, but it can easily be adapted for younger students. Also, this can be used as a "station" activity on the first day of school.

Station Directions: At this station I want you to think sincerely about what commitments you want me to make to you over the year and what commitments you will make to this class. Think bigger than just content. When you have taken time to seriously consider these commitments, please sign a contract. The contracts contain the list of things I'm committing to you to help you succeed in this class. On the contract, please sign under my commitments to you and add any you think are needed. Then list the commitments you will make and sign your name.

While the commitments need to come from you, here are some categories where a commitment on your part would benefit yourself and our classroom community:

- Behavior
- Work ethic
- Classroom community
- Self-advocacy
- Self-reflection

Possible commitment statement ideas (feel free to be more creative):

- I promise to treat my teachers and my classmates with the respect they deserve as human beings.
- I promise to be considerate of other people's ideas and beliefs.
- I promise to advocate on my own behalf and ask for help when needed.
- I promise to be honest with my teacher and myself even when I make a mistake.
- I promise to put forth quality effort in my classwork and homework.

CLASSROOM COMMITMENTS
CONTRACT

My commitments to you, my students:

- I promise to talk to and treat you as a human being and a unique individual.

- I promise to listen when you are speaking to me.

- I promise to work diligently to check in with you on a regular basis.

- I promise to help you to become the best version of yourself by pushing you to do more than you think is possible.

- I promise to help you reach outside your comfort zone in a way that feels safe and supportive to you.

Other personal commitment requests of the teacher:

Student commitments:

- I promise to treat my teachers and my classmates with the respect they deserve as human beings.

- I promise to be considerate of other people's ideas and beliefs.

- I promise to advocate on my own behalf and ask for help when needed.

- I promise to be honest with my teacher and myself even when I make a mistake.

- I promise to put forth quality effort in my classwork and homework.

_____
(student signature)

_____
(teacher signature)

_____
(date)

_____
(date)

Source: Reprinted with permission from Michele Sambiase (2021).

1

TOOL 3.6: Supporting Individual Students

When you experience challenging behavior from individual students, it is important to request assistance. This tool can be used to prepare for a meeting with your administrator to discuss how you can continue to support your student. Questions used in this tool will likely be asked by your administrator and can be considered as you determine appropriate interventions. Your mentor will be another valuable resource for sharing this information to discuss and brainstorm effective strategies. It is important to consider what your student does well as you consider interventions. Based on the information you share, your administrator might recommend additional support through a more formalized process, such as child study.

Student's Name:	Teacher's Name:
Student's Strengths: The strengths can be academic or nonacademic, but they reinforce the importance of a strengths-based approach.	**Student's Interests:** List things your student enjoys. These may be used to help determine motivation strategies.

Behavior(s) of Concern: Provide a summary of the behavior of concern. Describe when the behavior occurs, the frequency, duration, potential triggers, and what the behavior looks like in the classroom. Describe how the behavior is affecting the student or their peers in the classroom.

Interventions: Provide a summary of interventions you have tried and the impact of each.

Intervention:	Intervention:	Intervention:
Duration:	Duration:	Duration:
Outcome:	Outcome:	Outcome:

Parent Communication: Describe discussions you have had with the parents/guardians regarding the concerns and meeting outcomes.

Classroom Procedures and Routines

Establishing Classroom Procedures and Routines that Make an Impact

According to research, effective teachers establish rules, procedures, and routines as soon as possible, which even should take precedent over academic lessons during the first week of school (Stronge, 2018). And why is this important? Because teachers who spend time establishing and reinforcing reasonable, fair, and effective classroom procedures and routines at the beginning of the school year do not need to exert as much effort on similar tasks later on. In fact, these effective teachers seem to know that establishing good classroom procedures as early as possible in the school year is a proposition of "pay me now or pay me later," and it's better to invest now!

In our daily life, we incorporate procedures and routines to make our time use more efficient and productive. In our classrooms, procedures and routines communicate shared behavioral expectations and build a culture that values time on learning and student self-regulation. The benefits of having specific routines and behavior expectations in your classroom include the following key points (Hayes, 2020; Lester et al., 2017; Stronge, 2018):

- They decrease guesswork and add more predictability for students about what will happen.

- They add structure, framework, and patterns to classroom activities.

- They help students understand norms and consequences and be responsible for their own behaviors.

- They add more time for instructing and learning, rather than for organizing and disciplining.

- They result in less disciplinary incidents, higher student engagement, better learning habits, and less teacher stress.

 Words to Know

Procedure—a set of steps that establish a standard way of performing activities in the classroom

Routine—an activity or procedure that is repeated on a regular basis in the classroom

In sum, procedures and routines help take care of the more mundane aspects of classroom life. They also help students transition into class assignments with a minimal amount of explanation and lost instructional time. However, it's important to note that procedures and routines are only as effective as their implementation. To make them effective, you will need to teach, model, and enforce them with consistency (Lester et al., 2017). And, importantly, understand that

- Rules and routines that are owned by the students and not just the teacher become self-monitored and self-enforced;

- Clearer and fewer rules often are better than complex and more rules; and

- Do not create rules unless you intend to enforce them; no enforcement or inconsistent enforcement is the same as no rules.

⚒ Tools to Use

TOOL 4.1: Procedures and Routines for the Beginning of Class

You can easily lose 5–10 minutes in housekeeping and administrative tasks before the real learning starts at the beginning of a class, so setting procedures and routines is especially important for students to prepare for the classroom, quickly ease into the classroom routine with little wasted motion (and time), and move directly into the new learning for the day. Here are several important related points worth considering that can lead to a smoother and more efficient start to your class each day:

- **How will you greet students as they enter the class?** Will you stand by the door, greeting the students and collecting homework? Or will you sit at your desk and take care of some administrative duties while students place their homework in a designated box or basket? Both would work as long as you do it consistently and use the time productively.

- **If you use digital homework and assignments, how will students submit their work?** What will be your administrative procedures for using the platform? Are students trained on using the system? And do all students have access to the platform?

- **How will you record attendance?** Many schools use an online system to record student attendance. To make the entries efficiently, you would need to quickly learn students' names. If you are a high school teacher, you may teach a large number of students, and using a seating chart to mark off students may be faster.

- **If a student is absent, do you have procedures to help the student quickly catch up with the learning on their own?** Maybe you can select another student to be the "classroom helper" to share a notebook or folder with the day's agenda and learning materials with the absent student. Alternatively, if all materials are ready in advance, you can place them in a digital folder that the absent student can access from home.

- **How will seats be assigned to students,** and how will you make sure students know where to sit when they enter the class?

- **If you are an elementary teacher, you probably will need to take a lunch count. How will you do this?** (Pinterest.com provides some creative ideas to organize student names, such as using craft sticks, numbers, clothespins, Velcro, or magnets.) Whatever you do, make sure you have a system that is repetitive and as quick to manage as possible. The more time spent on lunch counts and the like, the less time spent on learning.

- **What will the students do while you are working on any required administrative tasks?** And what happens if the students arrive early? Consider having an entry assignment or preassignment ready every day.

- **To start off the learning, will you have "today's agenda" or "learning objectives"** written on the board and provide some opening warm-up activity for students while they are settling down? Some teachers have students recall the previous learning, review key vocabulary, answer trivia questions related to the learning, share a quote, or participate in do-now activities.

- **What will you do to ensure that textbooks, handouts, and other learning materials are available?** What would happen if some students forgot to bring their learning materials?

TOOL 4.2: Procedures, Routines, and Transitions During Class

Much of what you do as a teacher is management. It may seem trivial, but if you manage well, everything else will go much more smoothly. For instance, you need to manage supplies so that instruction can take place. Make sure you have considered all management items so that you have more time for instruction. This list of procedures, routines, and transitions comes with possible solutions to help you get started. In addition to these ideas, check with your grade-level or content colleagues as well as your mentor to see if there might be other procedures to consider.

1

What are the procedures for students to leave their seats during the classroom?	They may be getting supplies, getting a tissue, sharpening a pencil, or throwing items in the trash. If the lesson involves the use of computers, electronic tablets, or other equipment, what are the rules of using them and procedures to access them and store them when finished?
How will you handle student requests to leave the room?	Your school may already have a template hall pass. If not, create one. You can get crafty making your own nurse pass, office pass, library pass, and restroom pass. You can add a sign-out form by the passes for students to fill out their name, destination, time out, and time in. Don't forget to set a time limit for some passes such as the restroom passes. For younger students, using simple sign language to communicate their needs quietly might be helpful. • Make sure the students understand that they can only signal their request to leave when you are not teaching to the whole class. • Encourage students to use requests for restroom breaks and other reasons to leave the classroom very judiciously. • Build a routine for most breaks to occur at regular break time, therefore, cutting down on individual disruptions during the learning time.
How will you have the students transition from a whole-class activity into group learning?	One simple option is to have them turn to talk to the person next to them. You also can use other random grouping methods such as drawing student names from a hat, letting students choose colored index cards and grouping by colors, counting off by numbers, grouping by birthday months. Alternatively, if you want to group them by skill levels or interest, that will take more planning about procedures. Whatever the routine is, make sure it is as quick and easy as possible and that the students know it.

How will you let students know it is time to move from one activity to another?	One effective strategy is to use a timer to let students know how much time they have for a certain task. When time is up, they will be more prepared to switch to the new activity.
	When students transit from independent groups or group work to whole-class activities, you often need to get the entire class's attention. Set up a procedure to do this the same way every time so you don't need to yell to quiet students down. An effective way to do so is to use call and response.
	• The teacher says, "Macaroni and cheese!" and students reply, "Everybody freeze!"
	• The teacher says, "Hocus pocus!" and students reply, "Everybody focus!"
	• The teacher says, "Freeze! Everybody clap your hands," and students clap three times.
	• The teacher says, "Eyes and ears on me in 5-4-3-2-1," while holding up a hand to gesture the count down.

TOOL 4.3: Procedures and Routines for Class Closures

Equally important to having in-class guidelines is having closing routines and procedures. During the course of the class, students may have moved around the classroom and or worked on a variety of activities. It is then important for them to know what to do when they are done. Think through how you want to end your class. Use these tips to help you establish your closing procedures and routines.

- What will students do if they finish work early? Will you have a quick enrichment activity handy for them?

- How will you hand out and collect exit tickets for assessment purposes?

- How will you share information about homework? Make sure you provide time for students to ask questions and get clarifications.

- Will you have a set of closing routines for the students, such as the following?
  - ▷ Students summarize or reflect on what they have learned (e.g., "Using your own words, how will you explain to your parents what you have learned today?" "What are the most important things you have learned today?").
  - ▷ Help students think about the day's lesson and what comes next:
    - Make a prediction of what will be learned next.
    - Reflect and extend the lesson by connecting what students are learning and the real world around them.
    - Explore how students will use what they are learning 10 years from now.
  - ▷ A quick survey (such as thumbs up or down) to assess how students are feeling about the lesson and what they learned—whether they understand everything and are ready to move on, are kind of getting it but need more practice and help, or are not getting it at all and need lots of help.

- What are the routines for students to clean up and get ready for the next day's learning before they leave the classroom?

Welcoming Students on the First Day of School

Welcoming Students

Regardless of their age, welcoming students and ensuring they have a feeling of belonging has an important effect on academic success (St-Amand et al., 2017), and there likely is no more important time than the first day of school. How we treat our incoming students and families should be similar to how we welcome guests into our homes, so aim to make your classroom feel like a second home! Fostering a sense of belonging creates a welcoming and positive classroom climate, empowers students to explore who they are as individuals, supports their learning, ensures fairness and consistency in behavior management, and builds relationships (Chambers et al., 2017; St-Amand et al., 2017). So, make sure your students feel safe and comfortable in a clean, prepared, organized, and friendly space (Ford, 2005).

Words to Know

Belonging—a sense of emotional attachment to a place or group

Making a First Impression

The saying "you never get a second chance to make a first impression" is certainly applicable when it comes to the first day of school. The first encounter with your students is critical and can be used to set a positive and motivational tone for the entire school year. Most students will come to your class excited but apprehensive as a result of many unknowns (Anderson et al., 2011). They typically have questions such as "What is the teacher like?" "Will I have a lot of work?" "Will any of my friends be in my class?" "Will it be fun or boring, easy or hard?"

So where do you start? The answer to this question will differ from classroom to classroom based on the grade level, your philosophy as a teacher, and other considerations, such as the amount of time you will spend with the students each day. An elementary school teacher who has the same set of students from 8:00 a.m. to 3:00 p.m. will have a different approach from a high school teacher who has a block of 90–110 minutes, which will differ still from a middle school teacher who has a class period of

1

50 minutes. However, in all of these classrooms, the ambiance and feeling you create on the first day will carry through to the end of the year and have an impact on the overall effectiveness of the class (Anderson et al., 2011).

While there is mixed research on the effectiveness of how to address the first day, generally older students are more interested in knowing the course expectations, how information and delivery of the content will happen, policies and procedures, and personal information about the teacher and others in the class (Eskine & Hammer, 2017). These same topics or themes can be used with younger students but addressed at a more basic level. All kids want to know the rules, what and how they are going to be learning, as well as information about their classmates.

There are two general approaches to handling the first class and day with your students: 1) Is it more effective to go over all the typical first day items (organization, rules, etc.) immediately? or 2) Is it better to dive right into the content and engage students at the beginning, using the types of activities they will encounter in the class, such as talking, writing, thinking critically, problem solving, creating, collaborating, and leading? With respect to student motivation, positive instructor impressions, and positive student self-perceptions, the research is mixed, but there is some evidence that having a teaching activity may be more beneficial for the first class meeting as opposed to starting with a syllabus review (Anderson et al., 2011; Curtis & Moore, 2018). The following tools introduce ways you can combine the typical first day activities and also dive headfirst into learning concepts for your class.

🔧 Tools to Use

TOOL 5.1: Welcome Stations

This tool was designed with a high-school-level world history class in mind, but you can adjust it to meet your specific teaching needs. These station ideas can be used as stations, if the class period is long enough, or independently over the first few classes to help you build rapport with your students using techniques that will be relevant to the class content. Additionally, this is a good technique for ensuring students have an understanding and comprehension of your expectations as well as the high-level learning objectives and concepts. Each station speaks to what is important in welcoming students on the first day: building a relationship with the students (Station 1), letting students know the policies and procedures (Station 2), and empowering and motivating students to connect with the content (Station 3).

Note: If you would like to add another station, use the class contract information from Chapter 3 to help set the tone for student buy-in to the rules of the classroom.

Station 1: Evidence and Source Materials	In this class you will often use primary and secondary sources to analyze and synthesize information to answer questions. Since we are just getting to know each other, I thought a unique and interesting way to get to know me is using this technique. Dive deep into the documents provided to you about my life and examine not just the facts but the details you can learn, the inferences you can make, and the possible biases within the documents based on the creator of the documents. Use these documents to determine how Ms. Mitkowski is the same person she was as a child.
Station 2: Syllabus and Grading	• Read over the syllabus, which contains information on grading and my grading policy. • If you have any questions, submit them to the question box using the slips of paper provided or using the Google Form link provided. • Send a copy of this syllabus to your parents, either using email or a text photo. If you prefer, you can take a paper copy home so they can sign saying they received the syllabus. • After reviewing the syllabus, write down one topic you are excited about in this class, one topic you are unsure about, and one topic that seems to pique your interest.
Station 3: Personal Attributes	Every individual in this class comes with their own background, knowledge, interests, and personality. These personal attributes allow you to contribute to the class in a special and unique way. Consider your personal attributes and how they can help add value to our learning as a class. Consider the following: • What important events, background, customs, and beliefs are a part of your family history? • What major monuments, museums, or places have you investigated in books, using a computer, or seen in person? What did you learn about these places?

Station 3: Personal Attributes—(*continued*)	• Do you and/or your family have a connection to another country? If so which one(s)? Thinking about the world today, what scares you the most?
	• How has your family or personal experiences affected your opinions or viewpoints on things going on in the world or even in your neighborhood?
	• How have your experiences or family affected how you view historical events?
	• Would you have preferred to live during a different point in history? Explain.

Source: Reprinted with permission from Michele Sambiase (2021).

TOOL 5.2: Getting to Know You

This tool has a few activities or games you can use to start building relationships with the students in the class. While these activities are geared more for elementary students, they can be altered to be used in secondary grades. These ideas are just to get you started; as your class feels a sense of belonging, you can use these activities in different ways.

3-2-1	Have students write three things about themselves to share with the class, two things they are curious to learn this school year, and one question they have for the teacher. Students can then share aloud with the entire class, share in a small group, or just turn in the paper to you if they do not want to speak out.
Four Corners	Have students stand toward the middle of the classroom. Assign different topics, such as favorite ice cream. Then tell students whose favorite ice cream is vanilla to go to one corner, chocolate to another, swirl to another, and strawberry to the last corner. If students don't have a favorite or you don't list their favorite, they can stand in the middle. Then ask those students to tell everyone their favorite. Many getting-to-know-you topics can be used here to connect students to each other, and having them move in the classroom space gives them ownership.
Personal Attribute Bingo	Give students a bingo board with different attributes in each box. Tell them to move around and talk to each other to find someone in the class who identifies with that attribute. Let them know that they need to fill as many boxes as possible and can only use one classmate for each box. Examples include whether they have a pet, they have a sibling, art is their favorite subject, they play a sport, they enjoy reading, they speak another language, or they are excited to be in this class.

TOOL 5.3: Teacher Sharing

One of the most important aspects of the first day is getting to know the students and letting them get to know you. There are many ways you can choose to share information about yourself. For instance, you can make a PowerPoint presentation, you can talk to the class, or you can be mysterious and have hidden envelopes that the students find throughout the class period. The point is to find some way to let the students get to know you and be comfortable with you as a person. You are the teacher, but part of building the teacher-student relationship is sharing part of who you are with the students. This tool is a possible list of items you might want to share with your students.

Possible personal information to share with students:

- Who is your family?

- What activities or hobbies do you have?

- On a weekend, what is something you might do?

- Who has had a major impact on your life? What lessons did they impart?

- If you could have dinner with one person, who would it be?

- What is your favorite quote?

- Do you speak any foreign languages?

- What is something unique about you?

- Do you have a favorite sports team?

- What are some of your favorites (e.g., food, color, movie, book)?

- What is the greatest challenge you have overcome?

Building Relationships with Parents and Families

The Impact of the School-Family Relationship

So far in this part of the book we have discussed preparing for classroom life with your students. These next chapters offer suggestions for establishing another important relationship that affects your classroom: working with families. It is well established that positive parent/guardian interactions and perceptions of the school play an essential role in educational outcomes and experiences for students (Hampden-Thompson & Galindo, 2016). (Note: For the sake of brevity, the term parent(s) will be used to denote parent(s)/guardian(s) here and in subsequent chapters.) Yet, studies also show that new teachers are not always well prepared to work with families (Weiss et al, 2014). While teachers often find it uncomfortable reaching out to parents, research indicates that positive results are produced for students when the partnership between the school and family is emphasized (Jeynes, 2012). As a teacher, it will be important to your success and enjoyment of the job to have a positive relationship, not only with your students, but also with their families. While this relationship will grow and change over the course of the school year, being conscientious about building relationships at the beginning of the year will help as you may have parents contacting you early—and later—in the school year.

Building Relationships

How do you build this important school-family relationship? Often teachers must discuss information with parents that can be difficult to hear from the family perspective, especially regarding student academic performance or behavior concerns (Smith & Sheridan, 2019). The answer is pretty simple (although not so simple to implement): Make sure you create and sustain positive relationships, and then these conversations will be more productive and much easier. Teachers can begin to cultivate positive home relationships by developing trust and respect with parents (Flores & Kyere, 2020). Knowing how to communicate effectively and in a manner that is helpful to families will help build the trust and respect you seek. Specifically, a few ways you can establish a strong base of communication with families are

- Communicating frequently,

- Sending parents individualized information about students' performance frequently,

- Providing guidance on how to support students at home (Kraft, 2017), and

- Remembering to communicate positive news about students as often as possible.

The more frequently you communicate with families, the more adept you will be and the easier it will become.

⚒ Tools to Use

TOOL 6.1: Parent/Guardian Information Sheet

Having a solid communication strategy will help you develop good rapport with parents (Smith & Sheridan, 2019). To personalize your communication, you will need to know when and how to communicate (Kraft & Dougherty, 2013). This information sheet can be given to parents at the beginning of the school year so that you know the best way to contact them and when. The information sheet should be updated regularly as preferences may shift during the school year.

Parent(s)/guardian(s) name(s):
Parent(s)/guardian(s) address(es):
Best way to contact you (e.g., email, phone, text, written):
Best time to contact you:
Preferred language for communication:

TOOL 6.2: Family Communication Log

This log is a way for you to track your communication with parents and families. Keep an electronic copy of the log, and note that some schools require teachers to provide communication logs as part of their performance evaluation documentation. Because the log can help support teaching and learning in your classroom, it's worthwhile to examine the log every month and see where you can improve.

Date	Parent/Guardian's Name	Student's Name	Phone Call	Conference	Email	Written Note	Notes
12/16 4:10pm	Erin Altman	Piper Quinn	x				Spoke with Ms. Altman about how Piper is making an effort to participate more frequently. Let her know that at home she can help by continuing to encourage Piper to participate in class activities.

TOOL 6.3: English as a Second Language (ESL) Teacher Helpers

Communication can be especially tricky with ESL families, particularly if you are not fluent in the family's home language. It is important to see what resources for translation and communication with ESL families are available from your school.

Talking Points https://talkingpts.org	This site and app allow ESL or ELL teachers to communicate with families in their home language. You can send text messages in your language, and the parent/guardian will receive them in their home language. This app is free.
United Language Group https://www.unitedlanguage-group.com/	This site provides document translation and interpreters to help in communicating with families. Check to see if your school system uses this or another program to help with translation. This is not a free service, and this inclusion is not necessarily an endorsement of the products they provide. Rather, this is merely a good example of services that may be available to you.

TOOL 6.4: Business Card Template

Having a business card to give parents can be helpful for many reasons. Most professionals have business cards, so by presenting a business card you are demonstrating your professionalism to families. In addition, this small card will fit into wallets and purses whereas a handout may not. This tool is an example of what might be included on a business card. Obviously, you might not want to share your personal phone number, so you can share the school number where families can leave a message for you, or you can use technology apps like Google Voice (voice.google.com) or Remind (www .remind.com) that allow you to text and call from a phone number that is different from your own personal number.

> **Ms. Shabana Zaheer**
> 3rd Grade Teacher
> Simpson Elementary School
>
> **Contact Information:**
> Insert email address here
> Insert phone number here
> Insert class webpage here

Front of business card

> Please feel free to reach out to me through email, written notes, or a phone call. I will get back to you within 24 hours as it is important to me to work together for the betterment of your student.
>
> —*Ms. Zaheer*

Back of business card

TOOL 6.5: Communication Considerations

There are various methods of communication available to teachers to maintain a strong home–school relationship with families; however, some communication methods are more appropriate, depending on the nature of the conversation. Use this flow chart to determine the appropriate communication method for contacting parents/guardians.

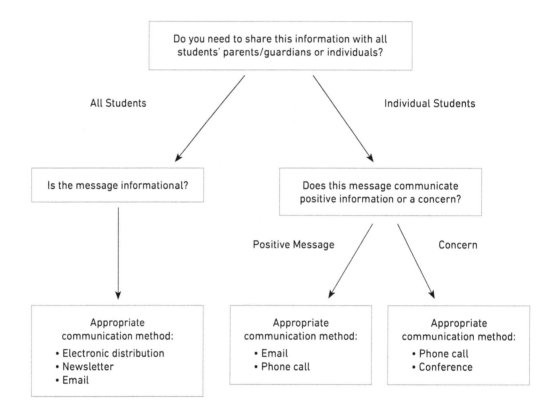

Hosting School-Family Events and Parent-Teacher Conferences

The Importance of Inviting Families into the Classroom

The importance of fostering the relationship between families and school has been the focus of legislation and teaching standards recently because this relationship plays a vital role in the climate of the classroom and student success (Jeynes, 2018). The Interstate New Teacher Assessment and Support Consortium (InTASC) Standards address this important relationship, including:

> 10(m). The teacher understands that alignment of family, school, and community spheres of influence enhances student learning and that discontinuity in these spheres of influences interferes with learning. (Council of Chief State School Officers, 2013, p. 45)

Additionally, in many U.S. states there is legislation in place to promote practices of family engagement through professional development (Ferrara, 2017). This is important as it has been found that parental involvement programs are consistently related to higher educational outcomes at all student levels from Pre-K through 12th grade (Jeynes, 2012).

Planned School Events

Given that parental/guardian involvement affects a students' academic achievement, there are certain times included in the school year to build the school-home relationship. In particular, events such as meet-the-teacher, back-to-school night, and parent-teacher conferences offer the opportunity to interact with your students' families. Because these events are planned, you have time to prepare for them and use them to your advantage. Research finds that not only are parental voluntary acts associated with positive educational outcomes for students but also school-initiated programs that encourage parental participation show positive educational outcomes for students

 Words to Know

Planned school events—events that are planned in advance and usually initiated by the school

(Jeynes, 2012). So even these events promote student achievement and, consequently, are important and should be well-planned.

Back-to-School Events

Back-to-school is always an exciting time for everyone, and often schools will create events to welcome students and families back to the building. These events can be the first time you interact with your students and their families. Figure 7.1 provides a list of possible back-to-school events your school may host, so check with a mentor teacher or trusted colleague on which opportunities are planned for families and how they operate.

FIGURE 7.1: Possible Back-to-School Events

Planned Events	Description	Helpful Tips
Meet-the-Teacher (sometimes called open house or orientation)	Meet-the-teacher is usually held prior to school beginning or early in the school year to allow students and their parents/guardians to meet the teacher, see the school, and become comfortable in the setting. There is no presentation for families, and the setting is rather informal. Families come into the school and move around as they choose.	• Dress professionally. • Have handouts, including information on how to contact you, ready to distribute. • Engage with the students if they come to the meeting.
Back-to-School Night (sometimes called open house)	Back-to-school night can be held prior to school beginning or within the first few weeks of the start of school. At back-to-school nights, parents/guardians often come without students to get more detailed information from the teacher about the curriculum, classroom expectations, and how to get to know the teacher. Typically, back-to-school night is more structured than meet-the-teacher. It often requires a presentation from the teacher, and parents/guardians have a schedule they follow.	• Dress professionally. • Be organized. • Build trust. • Give essential information. • Give your support for the importance of each learner. • Be positive and share a bit about yourself as a person. • Have handouts ready for families. • Have opportunities for parents/guardians to volunteer in the classroom or with classroom events.

Parent-Teacher Conferences

No school event brings as much anxiety for parents and teachers alike than conferences. Unfortunately, research shows that parents and teachers both find them to be stressful, treacherous, and sometimes traumatic (Pillet-Shore, 2016). Where do these negative feelings come from? In a conference, teachers may have to discuss critically and in detail with families about their student's work, behaviors, and attitudes. Parents can view this critique as a reflection on their parenting, and teachers can feel questioned on their competence as professionals (Pillet-Shore, 2016). So, how do you go about making the best of this situation? You plan! An easy way to start is to talk with veteran teachers on their experiences with conferences and some of the unexpected topics and conversations that may arise (Malinowsky, 2020). In addition, using the tips and conference form available here will help you feel less anxious and get you started on a positive path for your conference (see Tool 7.3).

🔧 Tools to Use

TOOL 7.1: Back-to-School Night Presentation

Back-to-school night is a time when you get to showcase your teaching craft. In order to do this in the most effective manner, you need to plan out the time and stay organized. Make sure you convey to families why you love to teach and why you chose to teach this grade or subject (Campbell, 2018). This outline can help guide you as you create your back-to-school night presentation, which can be created on PowerPoint or any other means that you choose. You will have only a limited amount of time for your presentation, so practice before the event.

1

Welcome to Back-to-School Night

Slide 2: Introduction

Introduce yourself (1–2 minutes).

- Your name
- Where you went to school
- What you like to do in your free time

Slide 3: Contact Information

Get parent contact information (2–3 minutes).

- Share with families the best time/way to contact you.
- Get contact information from parents (use parent contact information sheet).

Slide 4: Passion & Philosophy

Share your passion (2 minutes).

- Your philosophy of teaching and learning
- Why you like teaching
- Why you teach your specialized area (grade content area, ES, MS, HS, SPED, etc.)

Slide 5: Content Information

Examine content (2–3 minutes).

- Briefly touch on what will be taught and when during the year.
- Go over the details of the class schedule.

Slide 6: Expectations

Share Expectations (3–4 minutes).

- Go over class rules, processes, and (when needed) consequences.

Slide 7: Parents Help

How can parents help (3–4 minutes)?

- Give ideas or tools parents can use to help their student at home.
- Set up for volunteers if needed.

Slide 8: Answer Questions

Answer questions (5–10 minutes).

TOOL 7.2: Back-to-School Night Handout

This tool is an example of a handout you can send home with families that gives them quick access to core information about the school year. You can personalize the information to fit your grade level or area of expertise. Additionally, you can add information in the handout that you may not have put in your presentation.

Welcome to the 3rd Grade!

We hope you had a relaxing summer.

- Ms. Shabana Zaheer and Ms. Aria Rossi will be team teaching this year.
- Ms. Rossi teaches Language Arts, and Ms. Zaheer teaches Math and Content.
- Below, we have outlined some important information.
- This packet may not answer all your questions, so feel free to contact us at school.

Ms. Zaheer: (if you have a school number where families can call and leave you a message enter it here)

Insert school email address

Insert class webpage if you have one

Ms. Rossi: (if you have a school number where families can call and leave you a message enter it here)

Insert school email address

Insert class webpage if you have one

Language Arts

Language Arts consists of reading, spelling, writing, and English. This includes decoding words, sight words, oral reading, shared reading, and guided reading. Themed skills and diagnostic assessments also will be given throughout the grading periods. Nightly reading of 15–20 minutes is expected from each student.

Mathematics

Students will be using the math program, Everyday Math. It is a spiral program, which means that the material that students learn will be revisited sometime in the future. They will not be expected to master it the first time it is introduced.

Content

Students will have Science and Social Studies on an alternating schedule throughout the year. Homework will be given in these subjects as needed.

Homework Recorded in Planners

Students will have homework nightly. It should take students no longer than 30 minutes to complete without the nightly reading requirement. They will record homework to be completed in their planners before each class. Homework provides a way for you to be involved in your child's learning, so we ask that parents/guardians sign the student's planner each night, after checking that homework is completed. This will let us know that the student is keeping you in touch with our classroom activities. Please have your child attempt the homework, or at least the part that they understand. If they cannot finish a question, please make a note, so we know there was some difficulty in understanding.

Ms. Zaheer's Non-Core Classes
Lunch: Daily 11:38–12:08
PE: Daily 9:50–10:35
Music: Wed. 12:35–1:15
Computer: Fri. 12:35–1:15
Art: Thurs. 12:35–1:15

Ms. Rossi's Non-Core Classes
Lunch: Daily 11:42–12:12
PE: Daily 9:50–10:35
Art: Wed. 12:35–1:15
Computer: Tues. 12:35–1:15
Music: Thurs. 12:35–1:15

TOOL 7.3: Parent-Teacher Conference Tips and Self-Assessment

Since parent-teacher conferences can be the most stress-inducing times for new teachers, this tool offers tips and a self-assessment to help you be successful in your conferences (and, as a consequence, reduce your stress). In addition to these tips, make sure you talk with your mentor or another seasoned teacher to prepare yourself for conferences.

	Never	Rarely	Sometimes	Often	Always
Be Prepared and Plan Ahead					
I prepared an information sheet to share with parents.					
I have work samples to share with parents (in some cases having students choose samples can be appropriate).					
I am prepared with positive comments about the student and ways the student can improve.					
I prepared suggestions to help the student in the classroom.					
I plan for unplanned situations such as students attending when not expected, younger siblings being present, or surprising information shared by families to ensure I have appropriate and welcoming responses.					
Be Conscientious and Aware					
I am aware of the family structure of each student.					
I am ready to ask the parents and families for support and ways to help the student in the classroom.					
I know which family members will be attending the conference and how to properly address each one.					
I recognize that families address behavioral issues differently and am able to discuss behavioral management strategies used in the classroom.					

	Never	Rarely	Sometimes	Often	Always
Communicate Clearly					
I send parents a preconference questionnaire to help focus on parental concerns, if any.					
I do not use any educational jargon when communicating with parents.					
I use an interpreter or interpreting service (like Google Translate) to ensure clear and comfortable communication with families whose first language may not be English.					
I use specific examples when describing student actions in the classroom.					
I listen to parent concerns and questions.					
Be Professional and Respectful					
I dress in a manner that shows that I am a professional.					
I am welcoming and warm when families arrive.					
I sit with parents at a table or group of desks, not behind my desk.					
I am careful not to criticize parents or the way they choose to parent their child.					
I am respectful of everyone's time, always beginning and ending on time.					
I schedule a follow-up discussion if time runs out.					
I use an appropriate tone of voice and am polite.					
I show pride in my job and where I work by not speaking poorly of the school or my colleagues.					
I respect confidentiality and do not speak about another student in my conferences.					
I recognize when parents share delicate and confidential information with me, and I do not share it with others. Note: An exception is suspected child abuse, which most states mandate be reported.					
If I am still meeting with another family, I have a designated waiting area outside my classroom for families that arrive early.					

Source: Information from Ertel, 2020; Malinowsky, 2020.

TOOL 7.4: Parent-Teacher Conference Template

Use this tool to plan your parent-teacher conference. The tool will allow you to plan what items you will address with each family and give you a place to make notes on what was discussed. It also is a good idea to write a short thank you note or email to parents/guardians after the conference, reviewing with them what was discussed.

Student Name:	Date:
Class:	
Parents/Guardians:	
Student Strengths (show examples with student work):	Student Test Information:
Areas for Growth (show examples with student work):	Parent Concerns:
Grades:	Goals for the Student:
Plan for School:	Plan for Home:

Building a Constructive Relationship with Your Mentor

Why Do I Need a Mentor?

Teaching is a complex profession. And becoming an effective teacher takes continual improvement, effort, and support, especially in the beginning. Your first few years as a teacher will be vital in developing and refining your effectiveness as a teacher. Mentor teachers are one of the support systems put into place to help you with early success and sustained professional growth over time. In fact, it has been found that new teachers who have the support of a mentor teacher have higher satisfaction in their job and a higher commitment level to teaching (Ingersoll & Strong, 2011). Additionally, teachers who are provided a mentor in their first year are more likely to stay in the profession (USDOE, 2015). On a practical level, having a mentor teacher helps with teacher job satisfaction and retention—which is good for the school and good for you. Further, looking outside the benefits to the school and the teacher as an individual, students who have a novice teacher who is under the guidance of a mentor teacher have higher scores or gains on academic achievement tests (Ingersoll & Strong, 2011). Good teacher mentoring benefits everyone.

Who Is Your Mentor?

Here is an understatement: There is a big shift when you make the transition from your teacher preparation classes to the classroom. In fact, this kind of transition is one of the most critical in your teaching career (Jokikokko et al., 2017) as the reality of the profession begins to set in (Kane & Francis, 2013). To help with this critically important shift from being a teacher-in-training to being the teacher, a mentor who is an experienced teacher with practical knowledge of the teaching craft as well as professional knowledge can help you immensely. When implemented properly, your mentor teacher will be there to support, guide, and encourage you as well as give advice and feedback (Bressman et al., 2018) as you begin this important transition in the early stages of your teaching career.

Words to Know

Mentee—a teacher who receives mentoring from a more experienced teacher

Mentor teacher—an experienced teacher who has had success in the classroom and within the school setting, and is effective in their teaching craft

Mentoring—the process where a more experienced teacher offers support, guidance, feedback, advice, and encouragement to a novice teacher in order to support the new teacher's learning, professional growth, well-being, and transition from educational preparation to the real classroom (Bressman et al., 2018)

Novice/New teacher—a teacher who is just beginning their career as an educator

1

Building a Good Working Relationship with Your Mentor

Having a good working relationship with your mentor is essential for your growth and development as a teacher (Hudson, 2013), and knowing how to develop and nurture this relationship will be as important as the relationships you build with the students in your class. Your mentor teacher will have a large impact on your identity as a teacher (Izadinia, 2016), so this will be a significant relationship in your career. Communication through open and honest conversations will be vital. Through regular and clear communication you will construct a meaningful and mutually beneficial relationship for both you and your mentor, which will help you both to grow as professionals. You will bring new ideas and strategies just learned in your teacher preparation program, and your mentor will have ideas on how to help you implement these new techniques within the classroom. And they may even try to implement them in their own classroom!

🔧 Tools to Use

TOOL 8.1: Achieving a Positive Relationship with Your Mentor

This chart offers some strategies on which you can build a relationship with your mentor teacher in both your personal and professional life. Some of the strategies overlap and will help you in both spaces. In addition, the chart offers suggestions for possible conversation starters or different items to talk to your mentor about. These are just suggestions to use; you would need to make the topic specific to your needs as a teacher and the relationship with your mentor. If both of you work together using these strategies, you will both greatly benefit from the relationship.

Establishing shared expectations and strong relationships are valuable in maximizing opportunities for meaningful mentorship, and mentors and mentees should clarify a framework for collaboration that meets the mentee's needs and both individuals' schedules. (PEBC, 2016; Weinberg, 2021). Use this table to build relationships, discuss expectations, and ensure there is clarity about the frequency and purpose of your time together.

Professionally: • Share teaching strengths and weaknesses • Be receptive to feedback • Articulate expectations • Be reflective • Show professionalism • Share information and resources	• "I'm really confident in teaching small group reading, but I'm concerned about behavior management while I have my small group. Do you have any suggestions?" • "After watching me teach my lesson/looking at my lesson plans, do you have any feedback on how it could be better?" • "I'd really appreciate it if we could meet every other week for about 30 minutes just to touch base. Even if we just eat lunch together." • "Looking back at my reading lesson, I recognize that it went a little long and I started losing the kids' attention. Can you help me figure out a way to keep it short, but still ensure they understand?" • "My professional development last week was great. Have you heard about proactive management?"
Personally: • Build a personal relationship by sharing things about yourself • Have a positive attitude and smile	• "I really appreciate you taking the time to help me grow in my profession." • "My favorite thing about teaching is building relationships with the kids and watching them grow!"
Both professionally and personally: • Have open and honest communication • Be supportive • Display respect • Be a little vulnerable	• Anything in the other two conversation starter boxes. • "I like how you build your lesson plans." • "Since you came to watch me teach this week, do you think I can come watch you teach on my break next week?"

Source: Information from Hudson (2013); Liu et al. (2016); Izadinia (2016); Weimer (2018).

TOOL 8.2: Building a Relationship with Your Mentor

In order to help you achieve and maintain a positive relationship with your mentor, it helps to start small. The this-or-that tool can help you talk about your concerns or worries with your mentor as you begin your teaching journey. This list allows you to be vulnerable in admitting your fears but allows you to highlight your strengths. Additionally, you can ask your mentor teacher the same questions about their early teaching years and if their answers are different now. This too can help facilitate discussions that will help you build a strong foundation for your working relationship.

This or that: What is your biggest concern?

1

Parents	or	Kids
Behavior management	or	Lesson planning
Administration	or	Grade-level team
Special needs students	or	Gifted students
Teacher's lounge	or	Loneliness

TOOL 8.3: When Should You Go to Your Mentor for Help?

After building a solid foundation for your relationship with your mentor, you might be worried about when to ask for help. This chart gives you an idea of when your mentor teacher can help you.

When you...	Ask your mentor for help...
Have a question regarding curriculum, instruction, or assessment	• If you need help understanding the curriculum • If you are struggling with pacing • If all the lessons you think are solid during planning don't end up so awesome in the classroom • If you need help creating an assessment • If you need help looking at the data from an assessment
Have questions about behavior management	• If you have one student or a group of students who do not listen • If you are having trouble between students in the class • If you can't seem to get your class under control no matter how many different things you try • If you have a student you just don't "click" with
Feel isolated	• If you are having a hard time fitting into the school social network • If you are having a difficult time collaborating with grade level team members • If you are not sure if you are handling a situation in a professional manner • If you find yourself spending too much time alone planning • If you need a boost of confidence • If you need a friend who will just listen

When you...	Ask your mentor for help...
Need help with parents	• If you are having a hard time communicating with parents • If you need advice on how to set up your back-to-school night • If you need help structuring your conferences • If you need support after a challenging conversation with parents
Are setting up your classroom	• If you are finding it challenging to arrange your classroom because certain furniture can't be moved • If you need advice about seating arrangement
Need advice	• If you want to get a sense of what happens in an IEP or 504 meeting before your first one • If you want advice prior to going to child study for the first time • If you need a different perspective on any issue • If you need advice after an observation

Use this tool to schedule time with your mentor to provide instructional feedback when they observe your classroom. It may be useful to meet with your mentor prior to the observation to discuss what they will focus on during the observation. Remember that the goal of the observation is to have an opportunity to receive feedback and support from your mentor.

PART 2

Classroom Management and the Learning Environment

CHAPTERS 9–12

Create an environment that maximizes instructional time where students feel comfortable, safe, and engaged.

Seating Arrangement for Student Learning

┌─────────────────────┐

🔤 Words to Know

Flexible arrangement—the ability of a classroom seating arrangement to shift easily and quickly from one arrangement to another

Seating arrangement—the way in which a teacher decides to set the desks in the classroom

Traditional seating—having student desks arranged in rows and columns

└─────────────────────┘

Arranging Students for Success

"A good classroom seating arrangement is the cheapest form of classroom management" (Hamilton, 2019, p. 25). Every classroom, like every teacher and student, is unique, and all of their various personalities and needs are contained within this room. Teachers need to ensure the space they are given to perform their craft is arranged to maximize student learning and engagement—wall decorations, desk and computer locations, and more all make an impact (Hamilton, 2019). Arranging the classroom may mean that a teacher needs to look outside the traditional layout of desks and chairs in rows and columns and focus on individual needs within the confines of the space. Thinking "outside the box" with seating, being flexible in your classroom organization, and adjusting to learner needs will help keep students engaged (Hamilton, 2019); conversely students who are seated in the same arrangement for long periods of time can develop negativity for your classroom and even toward learning (Norazman et al., 2019).

It is also important to recognize that a student's individual characteristics may affect how they feel about a specific seating arrangement, thus influencing their learning engagement. For example, students who are introverted have been shown to demonstrate more creativity sitting in traditional rows, while extroverted students display more creativity in a cluster seating arrangement (Tobia et al., 2020). Therefore, recognizing students as individuals and focusing on their needs can feel like an art form (Tobia et al., 2020). Because classroom lessons and activities change on a daily basis, teachers should be adaptable when it comes to their seating arrangement, meaning that desk locations may be specific to the task for the day and the students in the classroom (Tobia et al., 2020).

Seating Considerations

It is the teacher's responsibility to manage the academic and social dynamics of the classroom, which becomes increasingly complex as the number of students in the classroom, along with their individual needs and preferences, increases (De Arment et al., 2013). Teachers have many reasons for placing students at specific locations in the classroom. The following list provides considerations that teachers commonly use when deciding seating in their classroom (Gremmen et al., 2016):

- Physical layout of the classroom and amount of space it contains

- Academic needs of the students

- Social needs of the students

- Personal characteristics of students

- Classroom efficiency

- Classroom management

- Preferences of students, parents, and administration

As you think about the full classroom configuration, you should consider balancing the need to create predictable patterns and stability with the benefits of variability. Using the considerations in the list above, many teachers prefer the traditional layout of rows and columns at the beginning of the school year to establish routines and order, but then they shift to small groups or a cluster layout later in the year to allow better cooperation among students (Gremmen et al., 2016). Cluster seating arrangement is great, but it affects learning if the class lacks order and discipline (Gremmen et al., 2016).

In addition to meeting the social dynamics of the classroom, the teacher must take into account what arrangement is best for the lesson (Norazman et al., 2019). If a science lesson involves groups of students working together on an experiment, cluster seating might be best. A history or social science lesson using interactive notetaking might benefit more from rows and columns. It's vital to recognize the needs of the lesson and how student seating can enhance or detract from learning.

Teachers make seating decisions based on their own considerations in the classroom, but consideration for student preferences can also be helpful. Students often know their strengths and weaknesses and have a valuable point of view. Looking at the various seating arrangements a teacher can create, students report that they feel most successful when sitting in two particular arrangements: rows and columns (independently) or in a cluster (Bickel, 2020). This shows that students also recognize that certain lessons lend themselves to different seating arrangements. Additionally, students note that peer support and easy access to resources are important (Bickel, 2020).

In summary, each seating arrangement has its pros and cons when looking at the needs of an entire classroom.

🔧 Tools to Use

TOOL 9.1: Questions to Ask About Classroom Seating

These questions should be taken into account when determining how to arrange the seats in your classroom.

Beliefs/ Philosophies	• Do you believe students learn better on their own or working cooperatively? • Do you believe it is important to use seating as classroom management? • Do you believe students' personalities impact their ability to work better independently or cooperatively? • Are you willing to change the classroom layout throughout the year?
Classroom Size	• What arrangement is going to work with the size and shape of the classroom? • Can multiple arrangements work within this space? • How can I arrange the space to allow for maximum student engagement and ease of access to needed materials for all? • Can the furniture in the classroom be moved easily?
Student Composition	• Which students work better alone/in a group? • Which students get distracted when in a group? • Do I have the proper procedures and policies in place to manage student behavior?
Lesson Planning	• Does the lesson I'm planning require students to focus on the task at hand or does it require cooperation? • Will students need to move around the room for this lesson? • What steps are included in the lesson plan to ensure students are all engaged if working cooperatively?

TOOL 9.2: When to Use Different Seating Arrangements

This chart can help you determine what type of seating arrangement to use for various classroom activities, lessons, and personalities. You can maximize student potential by changing seating arrangements to fit the needs of the lesson and learners.

Rows and Columns (Traditional)

- For helping to create and maintain order and discipline
- For tasks in which students should be doing their own work and not collaborating
- For students who might be more comfortable working independently
- For fostering independence and better confidence in students during the learning process
- For students who might be shy or have anxiety
- For a clear view of all students in the classroom
- For whole-group learning
- For teacher-centered activities and lessons

U-Shaped

- For classroom topics that require students to have classroom discussions or debates
- For activities or lessons when students might be asked to work with a shoulder partner
- For activities that require a large empty space in the classroom
- For more focus during a lesson
- For more space for the teachers' movement in the classroom

Pairs

- For activities that require students to work with a partner on a project or assignment
- For students who prefer working with a partner but not a group
- For a variation on the traditional seating but gives each student a partner
- For more teacher-centered lessons and activities

Clusters

- For developing interaction between student and teacher and between students
- For a group or team activity or lesson
- For cooperation during a lesson or activity
- For student-centered learning

Source: Information from Norazman et al. (2019).

TOOL 9.3: A Combination Seating Arrangement

This tool can demonstrate how a classroom might be arranged to meet the various learning and seating needs of your students and even adapted to various grade levels. This option works well for middle and high school teachers as different classes of students rotate in and out each class period. It may also help fit more students than a traditional seating arrangement if a class is too large or if one class is taking a test and the next is working in groups. For elementary teachers, it works well for students who might not always enjoy working in groups.

The arrangement combines cluster seating, traditional seating, and pairs seating. Whether students prefer to work independently, in small groups, or in pairs, they can use their preferred style. Additionally, students who are working independently can quickly and easily move their desks together to create a pair or join a small group if the lesson calls for it. Likewise, if a cluster arrangement is not working for a group of students, those students can quickly and easily move their desks apart to form rows and columns or separate into pairs. It also allows for easy movement and access to supplies and resources around the classroom.

The arrangement is flexible and adaptable, maximizing student engagement and learning, even if it doesn't necessarily encourage a quiet room or provide a lot of structure.

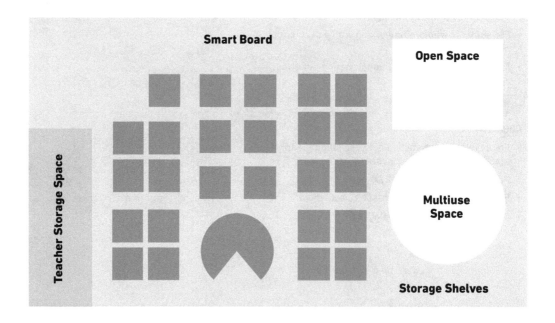

TOOL 9.4: Student Input for Seating Arrangements

For upper elementary and secondary students, you may wish to consider student input if you plan to reconfigure seating arrangements. This quick questionnaire can be completed as a bell ringer. It is designed for students to advocate for their own learning preferences and self-reflect on their own behavior. When using this tool, be sure you have modeled for students how to self-assess.

Student Name:
I currently sit beside/with:
This seating arrangement (circle one) **worked well** or **did not work well** for me because:
I work best when I sit (circle one) **individually** or **with a partner/group** because:
Other things to consider before rearranging desks:

Creating a Learning Atmosphere to Enhance Affective Learning

The Affective Learning Domain

As teachers, we often use the term "classroom community" when talking to others about our classes and our students. This community is built by the teacher in conjunction with the students, and helps students become 21st century learners who are ready to take on new challenges they may face, whether it be college, career, or life. To prepare students for this reality, teachers must ensure they integrate the cognitive, psychomotor, and affective domains of learning into their classrooms (Fisher et al., 2020a). In the past, the affective domain was overlooked because it can be a challenge to define, difficult to find effective ways to support, and problematic to know when and if a student has met the expectations (Casey & Fernandez-Rio, 2019). Yet, we know that affective learning conditions improve students' academic achievement (Green & Batool, 2017), which is one key reason why creating a classroom community that takes affective learning into account is important. As the world continues to increase in diversity and complexity due to technological growth, ease of travel, and so many more factors, it is more important than ever to ensure students are prepared not just in content and skills in English language arts, math, science, and social studies, but also in the ability to understand social interactions and the emotional responses that may come from these interactions, the responses that may come from these interactions, and how to deal with or react to various situations.

Affective Learning Affects Student Achievement

When Krathwohl and others (1964) first published their taxonomy of educational objectives, three domains were included. One of those domains was the affective domain, which deals with motivations, attitudes, and how to handle various difficulties daily. They included five sub-domains for affective learning: receiving, responding, valuing, organization, and characterization. All of these tenants of learning affect how students interact with the teacher, their peers, and the material they are learning. More recently, these sub-domains have been recharacterized to five core competencies:

self-awareness, self-management, social awareness, relationship skills, and responsible decision making (Dymnicki et al., 2013). These skills help students build important relationships in the classroom, control their reactions when academics may frustrate them, and make safe choices for themselves and their peers—all of which are skills that help students become life-long learners and productive members in society. The results from various meta-analyses have shown the impact of affective learning programs on academic achievement. Durlack and colleagues (2011) found that students who participated in an affective learning program showed significantly more positive results compared to their peers who did not participate in a similar program. The study also found that students in an affective learning program had significantly less distress and fewer behavioral issues. In fact, program participants gained 11 percentile points in academic achievement (Durlack et al., 2011). Since this seminal study, at least three additional meta-analyses have been conducted in which findings aligned with the Durlack study (Sklad et al, 2012; Taylor et al., 2017; Wiglesworth et al., 2016).

Student Learning Communities

It likely comes as no surprise that for students to be able to learn in any domain, be it cognitive, psychomotor, or affective, they must feel a sense of community and belonging. As the teacher, it will be up to you to create this safe and secure social learning community. A big question that this simple statement evokes is: How can you take a group of diverse learners with various skills and build positive affective attributes into the classroom learning community? One way is to use student learning communities (SLCs). While you might think that SLCs are just glorified cooperative learning groups or group work, it is more nuanced than that. These communities allow students to solve problems, offer insights, and help each other to develop new knowledge and skills within a structured framework (Fisher et al., 2020b). In order for these communities to flourish and for students to feel comfortable in their learning, the teacher must first create an environment where students can

- Engage in dialogue with their peers;

- Improve their self-efficacy; and

- Encounter different strategies for learning (Fisher et al., 2020b).

By encouraging this type of positive atmosphere, students will grow in multiple ways, and the classroom will be a place where the collective wisdom of the group will encourage the progress of individual students and of the group itself (Fisher et al., 2020a).

Tools to Use

TOOL 10.1: Incorporating Affective Learning into Your Day

Affective learning can help students gain the skills they need to function as productive citizens. While there are many ways to incorporate affective learning in the classroom, research suggests that effective programs typically incorporate four elements: *Sequenced* activities, *active* listening, *focus* on personal growth and social skills, and *explicit* focus on a certain skill to learn, or SAFE for short (Dymnicki et al., 2013). While these elements are part of a structured program that your school may or may not incorporate, there are ways for you to use these elements in your classroom.

 **Words to Know**

Collective efficacy —"The shared belief by a group in a particular learning environment that they have the knowledge, skills, and understandings to positively impact the outcomes of the experiences or tasks" (Fisher et al, 2020b, p. 5)

Self-efficacy —the feeling a person has about their ability to accomplish a given task

Sequenced activities	• Plan activities that are coordinated, connected, and sequential so as to ensure there is no uncertainty about what students are supposed to do, the order in which it will take place, and how they will know when they are finished. • Make sure activities are active and require students to be involved and not passive as they focus on developing these skills. • Examples include roleplay scripts that ensure each student has a role to play.

Active listening	• Model for students what active listening looks like:
	  – "What I think I heard you say is...."
	  – "Let me see if I understand you correctly...."
	  – "My understanding of what you said is.... Is that right?"
	  – "I heard you say... and.... Is that correct?"
	• Teach students these cues to use with others inside and outside the classroom.

Focus on skill development	• Each week choose a skill such as listening, controlling reactions, dealing with fears, etc. and have all your activities and active listening practice focus on that skill. • For example, if you are focusing on controlling reactions, you need to teach students how to react to challenging course material by understanding their response. Do they persist, give up, or crumple their paper? By recognizing their reaction, they can then problem solve what steps to take in order to move forward in their mastery of the topic.
Explicit focus on the skill	• If your skill development for the week is listening, then you need to come out and say, "We are going to be learning how to be good listeners" and focus your activities on that skill. • For example, in elementary school you might want to focus only on qualities of good listeners, and in middle or high school focus on how to be a good listener. Then create a short activity where students can practice that skill.

TOOL 10.2: Affective Learning Activities in the Classroom

Here is a starter list of SEL activities you might be able to incorporate into your classroom.

The teacher can	The student can
• Read books about problem solving and discuss what problem the character had and how they solved it. • Teach the difference between a fixed mindset and a growth mindset. • Use a quote or picture of the day to have students explain their interpretation of the quote or picture. What about it created that interpretation? Could one person interpret it multiple ways? • Discuss, create, implement, monitor, and evaluate SMART (**s**pecific, **m**easurable, **a**ttainable, **r**elevant, **t**ime-based) goals. • Have student check-ins each day (maybe while checking homework) to see how their day has been so far. • Model writing uplifting notes by having students focus on attributes such as kindness, honesty, trustworthiness. • Model writing from another person's perspective.	• Discuss books and characters' perspectives. • Learn the differences between growth and fixed mindsets and use growth mindset language. • Explain their interpretation of the quote/picture and why. • Create SMART (**s**pecific, **m**easurable, **a**ttainable, **r**elevant, **t**ime-based) goals. • Use check-ins to provide feedback to the teacher. • Write uplifting notes to each other in the class and use conflict resolution techniques. • Write a journal entry from another's perspective.

2

Using Proactive Classroom Management

What Is Proactive Classroom Management?

Often when you think of classroom management, you think of how you as the teacher will respond to students exhibiting external—and often disruptive or inappropriate—behaviors in the classroom. Your response might result in a public reprimand, which may embarrass a student, or be exclusionary such as an office referral (Cook et al., 2018). This type of management is reactive and can lead to unintended negative teacher–student interactions, lost instructional time, and an increase in the behaviors you are trying to eliminate (Cook et al., 2018). Proactive classroom management describes steps taken by the teacher *prior* to an incident, which can work to keep students engaged in their learning. Preventative classroom management refers to the actions taken by the teacher in order to anticipate and prevent classroom disruptions from occurring before they happen (Borich, 2006). Examples of proactive management include establishing the classroom rules and routines as well as a clear explanation of the consequences (Spoden & Fricke, 2018). This form of management requires the teacher to truly know and understand the students, organize and plan in such a way as to minimize student distraction, and then be conscious of students' activities during the course of a lesson (Spoden & Fricke, 2018).

Why Does Proactive Classroom Management Matter?

A significant number of teachers have reported that classroom behavior problems are a leading concern in their classrooms and that they need additional professional development and support in effective classroom management (Christofferson & Sullivan, 2015). Among the most common student behavior problems are disobedience and rudeness, talking out of turn, students getting out of their seat, verbal aggression, and over-activity followed by withdrawal, non-attentiveness, daydreaming, and idleness (Sun & Shek, 2012). When students display these disruptive behaviors in class they compromise instructional time, leading to an unproductive climate and a negative impact on student focus and learning (Cook et al., 2018). Obviously, effective classroom management is vital to student achievement. And using preventative and proactive management has been shown to positively affect student behavior (Larsen et al., 2018) and can be broken up into five separate categories (Cook et al., 2018; Lin, 2019; Nagro et al., 2019):

1. **Whole-group response:** This helps to create a positive classroom environment where all students have opportunities to respond frequently.
2. **Integrate movement:** This helps students to maintain focus and the ability to learn over a longer period of time.
3. **Visual strategies:** This strategy helps students by reducing anxiety and increasing predictability, so students know what to do, when, and how.
4. **Student choice:** This helps to engage students in their own learning.
5. **Building relationships:** This strategy helps create connections between the teacher/student and students, so they feel part of a team to work together.

Regardless of what type of preventative and proactive classroom management you choose to use in your classroom, the key to success is planning. These management strategies need to be considered during lesson planning so that you are ready with the proactive discipline strategies that quickly and successfully minimize students' behavior disruptions and maximize teaching and learning time. Remember: Even the best teachers will have student discipline challenges, but the secret to success is learning to quickly and adeptly handle the disruptions and, ultimately, creating a classroom environment in which students want to learn and behave appropriately.

⚒ Tools to Use

TOOL 11.1: Classroom Management Categories and Strategies

This planning tool can help you prepare your lessons using the five categories of proactive classroom management. If you are trying to implement preventative and proactive management, you can glimpse at this chart and use some of the strategies (broken up by categories) in your plan. See Tool 11.2 for a lesson plan incorporating some of these strategies.

2

Whole-Group Response	Integrate Movement	Visual Strategies	Student Choice	Building Relationships
Increase ability to respond with • Choral answering • Choral reading • White boards • Closed-ended questions • A digital response system, such as Kahoot! • Interactive notebooks	• Pointing • Tracing • Gesturing • Snapping • Clapping • Acting out • Dancing • Providing brain breaks • Using manipulatives • Changing locations	• Schedule • First/then board (see Tool 11.3) • Label items in the room to help students stay organized. • Having an organizational strategy for classroom items gives visual cues as to what is expected. • Arrange the classroom environment in a way that focuses attention and to set boundaries. • Have a consequence poster explaining the consequences for various choices.	**Give students the ability to** • Decide which activities to do first. • Determine how to engage in the lesson. • Decide what product to produce for assessment. (Student choice can be put into daily routines and interactions with other students.)	**Create connections by** • Greeting students at the door. • Giving behavior contingent praise. • Anticipating when students will struggle with content and have misconceptions. • Correcting student behavior prior to an infraction. • Using teacher proximity. • Practicing transitions and routines.

Source: Information from Nagro et al. (2019); Cook et al. (2018); Lin (2019).

TOOL 11.2: Integrating Preventative Classroom Management Categories

One of the best ways to use proactive and preventative classroom management in your classroom is to build it into your lesson planning. While this might seem tedious as you begin, the impact will be seen in student on-task time and decreased behavioral interruptions. This chart can be created prior to writing your lesson plan to ensure you include some of the preventative classroom management categories throughout your lesson. The chart also allows you to see if you are overusing a category. In the chart you can see the different parts of the lesson and where the teacher intends to integrate preventative classroom management into the plan. After filling out this chart you can easily take the different items and copy and paste them into the lesson plan format of your choosing. Many of the suggestions here will be things you may already include in your lesson plans; however, it will pay dividends to be thoughtful and intentional and ensure these aspects of proactive and preventative classroom management are included in your planning.

Lesson Structure	Plan	Whole-Group Responding	Visual Strategies	Movement	Student Choice	Build Relationships
Standards and Objectives	The student(s) will solve single and multistep problems using addition and/or subtraction of decimals.		• Standards and objectives are posted • Rules and procedures are posted.			
Greet Students at the Door						Teacher gives high fives, welcomes, and smiles.
Stage 1: Introduction (Orientation) (Greet students at the door while others do WYW.)	While you Wait (WYW) • Decimal crossword puzzle • Triangle puzzle	Students share with a partner what they chose to do and how they solved the puzzles.			Students can choose which activity to complete while they wait.	Students are immediately engaged in a planned learning activity.
Stage 2: Main Lesson Presentation (Whole-Group Instruction)	After reviewing both puzzles, teacher will work through decimal word problems together with students.	Students use white boards to give their answers.	Use the poster with the steps for solving word problems to help guide students through the problem.	Act out the first problem together as a class.		Teacher uses proximity to monitor and prevent any possible disruptions.

Lesson Structure	Plan	Whole-Group Responding	Visual Strategies	Movement	Student Choice	Build Relationships
Stage 3: Practice (Small-Group Instruction and Centers)	Pull small groups back based on what was seen/heard while rotating during whole group.		• Students use individual copies of the steps for solving a word problem as they work in small groups. • Rules & procedures for playlist work are posted.	• Students not in small group will move to work on playlist items. • Students in small group will use manipulatives to help solve the problem.	Students not in small group will complete their playlist. (See example in Tool 11.4.)	• Teacher reviews procedures and rules for working on playlists. • Teacher works with small group helping students together and individually on the work.
Lesson Summary and Closure	• Students will share out what they worked on during small group. • Students will complete an exit slip.	Choral responding		Students move back to their seats after working on playlist items.		

Source: Information from Nagro et al. (2019).

TOOL 11.3: First/Then Board

A first/then board is a visual strategy that you can use to increase predictability and learning structure for students. The idea behind the first/then board is that students are asked to do a less-preferred activity followed by a preferred activity. There are many ways to create a first/then board. We have provided an example from a high school visual arts class. The student has to first complete an activity that requires them to analyze and interpret art, and then they create their own art. While this example was created for a specific student in mind, you can create and change it for your class as a whole or for particular students. By putting the less-preferred activity first, students are motivated to get the work done so they can then move onto the more desirable task. Make sure the tasks in the *first* section are able to be accomplished so that students have time to get started on the *then* section.

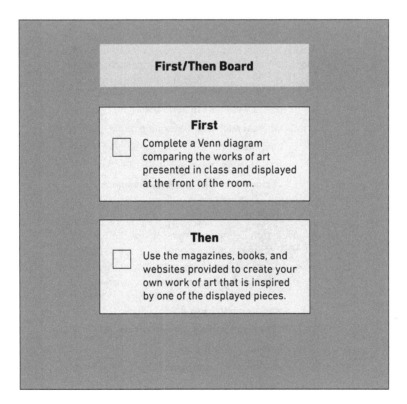

2

TOOL 11.4: Student Playlist

The student playlist is a way to give students choice in completing classwork. Students are given must-do activities for the week and then given the choice of when they complete them. If students complete must-do activities, other activities they *may do* are available. Playlists can be personalized to individual students, small groups, or the entire class. Playlists can be done daily or weekly. (Note: The sample below is an example of a weekly playlist). Playlists can be similar to first/then boards, but they also can introduce student choice into the activities. For students who need more structure and help with executive function, a first/then board may be more appropriate.

Sophie's Playlist

• • •

Must Do: After each group lesson, you must complete a must-do, then you can complete a may-do.

☐ Math Lesson 3.4 in math book
☐ Decimal addition/subtraction game
☐ Find the error
☐ Math around the room
☐ Decimal problem-based assessment

May Do: After completing your must-do for the day, you may complete any may-dos. In order to ensure everyone gets a chance, remember you may not repeat a may-do throughout the week.

☐ Math computer program
☐ Create and solve your own problems
☐ Decimal pattern game
☐ Multiplication war game
☐ Math book p. 51

Ensuring Your Classroom Is a No-Bully Zone

The Bullying Problem

Sadly, bullying is a worldwide problem in schools and classrooms. In the United States, the Center for Disease Control (CDC) reports that 1 in 5 high school students is bullied on school grounds and that approximately 30 percent of middle school students experience bullying (CDC, n.d.). That is a staggering number! So, what exactly is bullying?

> Bullying is any unwanted aggressive behavior(s) by another youth or group of youths who are not siblings or current dating partners that involves an observed or perceived power imbalance and is repeated multiple times or is highly likely to be repeated. Bullying may inflict harm or distress on the targeted youth including physical, psychological, social or educational harm. (Gladden et al., 2014, p. 7)

Knowing what bullying is and what bullying is not is essential in preventing it from occurring in your classroom. In fact, teachers play a vital role in the detection and prevention of bullying (National Institute of Justice, 2020). However, teachers often feel like bystanders and are unsure of when, how, and if they should intervene in a possible bullying situation (Smith-Adcock et al., 2019; Pas et al., 2019). In addition, teachers have a lot on their plates professionally, and often the focus on those responsibilities supersede the focus or concern about bullying (Waters & Mashburn, 2017). With all these responsibilities, how does a teacher address something as critically important as preventing bullying?

Preventing Bullying in Your Classroom

Students would prefer not to involve adults in a bullying situation and choose to handle it in a different way, but when teachers do get involved, there is a substantial reduction in the continuation of bullying (Rigby, 2020; Waters & Mashburn, 2017). And for those students who are being bullied, ensuring our classrooms are bully-free zones is important to their physical, social, emotional, and academic well-being. We know that relationships between you and your students, as well as among students, are important,

---

Words to Know

Defending behavior—behavior a student engages in to defend themselves or another student who is being bullied

Power imbalance—"the attempt by the perpetrator(s) to use observed or perceived personal or situational characteristics to exert control over the targeted youth's behavior or limit the victim's ability to respond or stop their aggression" (Gladden et al., 2014, p.8)

and children are affected by their classmates and the climate that is created in the classroom (Sentse et al., 2015). As a teacher you set the tone for your classroom and if you don't address negative behaviors when they happen, that sends a signal to the students that it is OK to continue to behave in that manner. In fact, your students need you to create a strict but fair classroom when it comes to the rules and then hold them to high expectations on how they treat others while you continue to build a warm, caring, and supportive relationship with them (Thornberg et al., 2018). Interestingly, classrooms that have this supportive-cooperative climate and a teacher who uses strategies to build this climate are more successful in dealing with bullying in the long run than a classroom that is authoritarian (Wachs et al., 2019). This all seems like a tall order, but by building these relationships and having proactive behavior management in place you are stopping the victimization of students and increasing the likelihood that other students will defend their bullied classmate (Thornberg et al., 2018).

🔧 Tools to Use

TOOL 12.1: Identifying Bullying

As stated above, teachers play an important role in helping students deal with bullying situations and in implementing anti-bullying strategies and policies (Waters & Mashburn, 2017). In order to successfully fulfill an anti-bullying role, it is important for teachers to be able to identify different types of bullying behavior (although research suggests teachers often struggle to do so) (Pas et al., 2019). This tool reviews some of the basics of bullying, such as how it occurs and how to help you feel more confident in determining if a situation is bullying or just kids being kids. This tool also should help you as you talk to your students about bullying. In addition, the school counselor is a good resource for information above and beyond what is found in this tool.

2

🔤 Words to Know

Victimization— being the target of aggressive or bullying behavior by others

Modes of Bullying	**Direct:** an act that is done directly to an individual, such as name calling, hitting, hurtful writing, etc.
	Indirect: covert bullying that is not done directly to another's face and might include spreading hurtful information about another
Types of Bullying	**Physical:** use of physical force to harm another such as hitting, kicking, spitting, tripping, pushing, and punching.
	Verbal: use of words, either oral or written, to cause harm, such as intimidating written notes, taunting, name calling, sexual harassment, or offensive hand gestures.
	Relational: acts done to harm another's reputation and or relationships, such as spreading false and harmful rumors, writing hurtful comments in public spaces, sharing embarrassing or harmful images, either electronically or physically, without permission.
	Damage to property: causing harm or damage or making modifications to another's property with the intent to cause harm; this can include taking someone's property and refusing to return it, ruining someone's property in front of them, and deleting a person's information on an electronic device.
	Psychological: manipulating how others think by causing individuals to question their own memories of an event that took place or the way they are perceiving or judging situations or events.
	Electronic: using electronic devices to bully another through words, pictures, or spreading false gossip.
Where Bullying Occurs	• At school, especially between classroom settings, in restrooms and on playgrounds, in the lunchroom, and in other less supervised areas • At school events such as school dances, sporting events, or arts performances • Going to school or home from school • In the neighborhood or on the street, especially as a follow-up to events that originated or occurred at school • On the internet, via social media, or in private messages • Text messages

Source: Information from Gladden et al. (2014).

TOOL 12.2: Strategies to Prevent Bullying in the Classroom

The best defense is a good offense, right? There are strategies you can use within your classroom to help prevent bullying. This tool lists some strategies that can help as you work to identify and prevent bullying.

Teacher's Responsibility:

- Hold regular class meetings
- Teach students to be self-aware and reflective
- Conflict resolution
- Emphasize accountability
- Apply rules fairly and consistently
- Give advice when needed
- Be a resource to students

Students' Responsibility:

- Hold themselves accountable
- Follow rules consistently
- Be peer advocates

Shared Responsibility:

- Value kindness
- Emphasize empathy
- Create classroom rules
- Develop a relationship with the school counselor
- Develop teamwork
- Involve parents

Source: Information from David-Ferdon et al. (2016); Olweus (1993); School Specialty (2018); Smith-Adcock et al. (2019); United States Government (n.d.).

TOOL 12.3: Creating a Warm and Caring Antibullying Climate

When it comes to bullying, it is important to note that bullying is likely to occur in classrooms with a poor climate and a strong status hierarchy (Saarento et al., 2015). To create a space that does not have this hierarchy and where the climate is warm, caring, and safe, building relationships with students and among students is important. In addition to preventing bullying, building positive and supportive relationships will help other students stand up and say something if they see bullying taking place (Thornberg et al., 2018). This tool will help you self-assess whether you are creating a classroom that is warm, caring, supportive, controlled, cooperative, demanding, and cohesive—all factors that help with antibullying (Thornberg et al., 2018; Wachs et al., 2019).

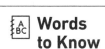

Words to Know

Status hierarchy —a social construct that is built upon the idea that some people have a higher status than others due to a variety of factors

2

Have I had a one-on-one conversation with each of my students about something nonacademic?	Yes	No	If no, how can you fit this into your schedule?
In addition to learning outcomes, do students know I recognize and see the effort they are putting forth?	Yes	No	If no, consider focusing positive comments on student effort.
Do I make connections in my lessons to current topics of interest to my students?	Yes	No	If no, think about how you might incorporate some pop culture into your lesson or tie it to a real-life situation the students are facing.
Do I model the respect and social skills I want to see from my students?	Yes	No	If no, could you think aloud the next time you get frustrated and model for students how you self-regulate?
Have I set classroom rules that are appropriate, understood by all, and enforced fairly?	Yes	No	If no, it might be time to hit the reset button and discuss with the class that things aren't working out and the class may need to reset and start again with the rules. To prevent this problem, spending ample time at the beginning of the school year is key to designing and enforcing the rules. With good classroom rules for behavior toward others, you are providing structure.
Am I happy to come to work every day?	Yes	No	If no, your students will feel that attitude and will respond accordingly.
Do I create engaging lesson plans with my students in mind?	Yes	No	If no, recognize that students can tell when lesson plans are thrown together and when they are well thought out with them in mind.
Do I hold class meetings or morning meetings regularly with my students?	Yes	No	If no, consider adding this once a week or biweekly as it gives time to get to know the students and for them to get to know each other. This also could be a time to work on team building, conflict management, and social-emotional learning.
Do I use cooperative learning and encourage students to work together?	Yes	No	If no, consider using this instructional strategy to help build relationships between students.
When an aggressive or bullying behavior occurs, do I respond immediately with proper intervention and firm resolution to the behavior?	Yes	No	If no, make sure you know what is bullying behavior, be keenly aware of any such behavior, and intervene quickly if it should occur.

PART 3

Instructional Planning

CHAPTERS 13–19

Plan for success and with confidence to ensure your students get the best instruction possible.

Getting a Grip on Lesson Planning with the Curriculum in Mind

What Is Curriculum's Purpose?

ABC Words to Know	

Words to Know

Curriculum—the standards, activities, books, resources, tools, and interactions that help a student grow and learn

Pacing guide—a guide given to help determine how much time should be spent on a topic or unit

Scope—the depth at which curricular items should be taught

Sequence—the order in which curricular items should be taught

What should students know? What should students learn? What will help students succeed the next school year? What will help students to be productive citizens when their schooling is complete? Curriculum tries to answer these questions. Curriculum is purposeful and central to the school experience (Richmond, 2018). Additionally, curriculum is wide, complex, and it matters.

As a teacher in your first or early years of teaching, you may have walked into your classroom ready for all the excitement of preparing the room for your students, organizing the desks, decorating the walls, and preparing your first lessons. What you might not have expected are the numerous curriculum guidelines and materials you found waiting for you: the standards of your state and school district, the textbooks and numerous teacher's manuals, the scope and sequence for the content areas you will be teaching, the pacing guide, and the many items other teachers passed down to you that they use. So, what do you do with all this material? What is critical? How do you make sense of it all? While all these forms of curriculum exist, curriculum is more than just these documents and words on a page; curriculum is what takes place in your classroom daily through instruction. Being knowledgeable of the curriculum is important so you can create lessons and activities for your class, which are curriculum-based (Süral & Dedebali, 2018).

Getting to Know Your Curriculum

So, where to start? One good answer to this question is the curriculum standards. Each educational entity, be it at the national level (Common Core of Learning), the state, the district, or in some instances, the school, have developed standards for what students should know and be able to do by the time they leave your classroom. There are at least three levels of curriculum you should become well-acquainted with in order to ensure you are adequately prepared to begin planning quality and engaging instruction (see Figure 13.1).

To begin, ensure you are familiar with national standards to guide your content area. For instance, in science, you should be familiar with the process standards from the National Center for Science Standards (NCSS) or, in math, the National Council for Teachers of Mathematics (NCTM). Curricular standards will differ by content area.

Next, you will need to acquaint yourself with your state standards. As a teacher, you should understand the relevant knowledge, skills, and vocabulary students should possess in order to demonstrate mastery of state standards. This is especially important because most states have proficiency tests based on these standards. Additionally, analyze the verbiage of your state standards to determine the cognitive demand delineated within each standard.

Finally, your district planning guides, which may include a pacing guide, will likely determine when you plan and deliver the day-to-day instruction. While the planning guide contains the standards, its main focus is to help you understand when in the school year to teach these standards and for how long. In addition, the planning guide may include standards from the grade level above and below the grade you are teaching so that you can see the standard progression from year to year. This will also give you an idea of what students should know already and the depth at which you should explore the topic. Many planning guides specify benchmarks for when content should be covered and even include benchmark assessments to assess student progress.

In addition to specifying when certain content should be taught, planning guides often provide information about what resources are available to support the instruction for content. Looking at the three levels of curriculum can provide information on what you should consider when lesson planning.

National Standards

- What national standards guide quality instruction in this content area?

- What standards guide instruction on specified populations (i.e., ESL, gifted, students with disabilities)

State Standards

- What are the essential knowledge and skills in the curriculum?

- What key vocabulary is used?

- What cognitive demand is delineated in the standards?

- How will students be assessed?

3

District Pacing Guides

- What differences (if any) are there between the state curriculum and district curriculum?

- When will you teach specific content?

- What opportunities exist for cross-curricular instruction based on pacing guides of other content areas?

- What benchmark assessments (if any) are there to formatively and summatively assess student learning?

- What resources are available to support instruction?

Once you consider the curriculum standards, you can consider the other curricular tools to help you. Think of the curriculum materials as tools provided to support student learning (Dietiker et al., 2018). The longer you teach, the easier it will become to understand the multilayered curricula and put the curricula to work in your classroom (Lim et al., 2016).

Planning Initial Lessons

Curriculum plays a critical role in planning your lessons, and it guides us to ask this essential question: What do you want students to know or do as a result of the lesson? In a sense, you are thinking of the outcome before the actual lesson. As you plan your instruction, you will have many factors that influence your plan for delivery. Figure 13.1 gives a visual of the process of planning and the various considerations that affect planning decisions. To break down some of those considerations, understand what each term means, determine what questions to ask yourself at each step, and examine the following items:

- **Curriculum:** What essential knowledge and skills should be included?

- **Pacing guides:** When will I plan this instruction and what resources and cross-curricular opportunities are available for students?

- **Objective:** What do you want students to know or do?

- **Background knowledge:** What do students already know about the content? What preassessment information will I have to guide instruction?

- **Resources:** What resources do I have at my disposal to reinforce content? What additional resources do I need and where can I get them?

- **Instructional methodology:** What instructional strategies will support high levels of student engagement and meet the curricular objective?

- **Time frame:** What is a realistic timeframe for content delivery?

- **Assessment:** How will I know if students mastered the material? How will I plan for both formative *and* summative assessment?

FIGURE 13.1: Lesson Planning Considerations

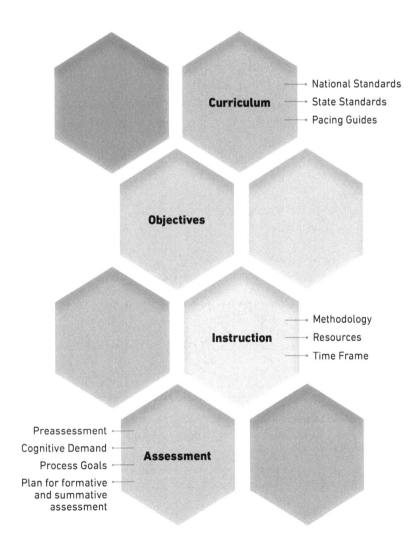

Tools to Use

TOOL 13.1: Planning Template

Now that you are aware of all the pieces of curriculum and considerations for planning, it is time to sit down and plan the first two weeks of school. What lesson plan format should you use? Your school or district may have a template you are required to use; if so, then, of course use it. If you get to determine your own planning template, make sure you apply it flexibly to your own setting (Johnson, 2019). The following lesson plan template focuses more on direct instruction and its major steps: introduction, presentation, and practice. This lesson template can help organize your lesson around these direct instruction components. For more information on how to effectively implement differentiated instruction, see Chapter 18.

Note: This approach is closely akin to the best elements of direct instruction. Of course, there are many other instructional strategies that can and should be considered in a quality instructional unit.

Teacher:

Date:

Subject/Content:

Standard(s) Addressed: This section of the template helps you plan what the students should know at the end of the lesson. Additionally, this gives students an idea of where you expect them to end up by the end of the lesson. Your objective should be derived from the standard(s) for your state, district, or school.

Materials: List your materials or resources here, so you know you have everything needed for the lesson.

Stage 1: Introduction (Orientation) – Captures student attention; clarifies learning objectives and student expectations

Anticipatory Set: The Hook – Strategies to motivate students to engage in this lesson including activating prior knowledge

Learning Objective: As a result of this lesson students will demonstrate their knowledge of
_____ in the following way(s):

Lesson Intention: Articulating the learning intention from the student's perspective: student-friendly language, including purpose and/or connection to the real world. Students need to know what is expected of them. The intentions can be stated and if required by your school written daily in the classroom.

Today I will learn...
I can...
This is important because...

Stage 2: Main Lesson Presentation – Explains the new content or demonstrates a new task or concept. This is what we traditionally think of as "teaching."	
Task(s)	**Description**
Model Procedures Using Appropriate Instructional Strategies Show the students the skill or concept, so that they can see it in action.	
Provide Examples	

Stage 3: Practice – Uses gradual release of teacher control as students transition from guided practice to independent practice; checks for understanding and provides feedback		
Guided Practice, Formative Assessment and Feedback You will ask questions, observe students, or use other techniques to check for student understanding. Students will be implementing the knowledge or skills explained and demonstrated on their own, while you supervise. You can use the information gleaned from the feedback to help students.	**Activities**	**Questions to be asked during this activity**
Independent Practice Students implement on their own without your supervision.		
Lesson Summary and Closure		
Assessment of performance, opportunities for retention and transfer of learning to novel tasks This section should include well thought-out formative (ongoing) and summative (outcome) assessments, as needed. Focus on what you want to see from students. You can adjust your guided practice based on the checks. You can include the independent practice as a follow-up instructional strategy.		

Other Considerations—things to think about as you plan your lesson
Homework Will students have practice to complete at home? What does the homework look like in terms of connectivity to the in-class learning? Can students successfully engage in the homework by working independently? Does the homework differentiate for advanced or struggling students? Is the amount of time required reasonable for the age and ability of the learners? What will you do with the homework? Remember: The real value in homework is the guided feedback that students receive.

Source: Reprinted with permission from James Stronge, 2021.

TOOL 13.2: Curriculum Needs Chart

The following chart will help you assess if you have all the necessary pieces of curriculum from which to develop your lesson plans. Each of these tools is critical to ensure your success, especially so in the first years of teaching as you are learning the curriculum and how to apply it. If you have not found these items, your school administrator or mentor teacher would be a great resource!

	I have found this information.	I am not sure where to find this information.
I know the district's calendar for the school year.	☐	☐
I know what the state and district have set as curriculum guides.	☐	☐
I know the sequence of the subject matter.	☐	☐
I know the scope of the subject matter.	☐	☐
I know the essential understandings for student learning.	☐	☐
I know what students should know and be able to do at the end of each unit.	☐	☐
I know the local standards.	☐	☐
I know the pacing guidelines.	☐	☐
I know the available teacher's manuals and resources.	☐	☐

TOOL 13.3: How to Plan for the First Month and First Grading Period

This step-by-step design was created to show you how to map out your curriculum with your initial lesson plans. While the first grading period will be longer than a month, this gives you a good starting point for future weeks in the grading period. Once you have set your personal goals, started developing a lesson plan, and have located all curriculum materials needed, you can use this tool to map out your grading period. These simple and practical steps should help you be more confident in beginning the school year with a lesson plan in hand!

Grading period #1 — 47 Days

Monday	Tuesday	Wednesday	Thursday	Friday	Saturday	Sunday
		1	2	3	4	5
		Unit #1				
6	7	8	9	10	11	12
		Unit #1				
13	14	15	16	17	18	19
	Unit Review	Unit #1				
20 No School	21	22 Unit #1 Assessment	23 Unit #2	24	25	26
27	28	29	30	31		
		Unit #2				

1. Get a monthly calendar.
2. Get the grading period breakdown from the school calendar.
3. Examine the pacing guide provided by your organization.
4. Create broad unit plans for the first grading period and add them to the calendar.
5. Include unit reviews and assessments.
6. Write two weeks' worth of daily lesson plans using teacher's editions and supplementary materials.

14 Planning Engaging Opening and Closing Activities

Opening and Closing Activities Leave an Impression

A good lesson plan is like a good book; the opening is engaging and leaves the reader wanting to know more, the middle is the meat of the book where the bulk of events happen, and the end of the book brings it to a nice close. Similarly, lesson plans should have openings and closings to enhance the lesson. The opening and closing activities should be about 5–10 minutes and can roll into the main lesson or give the main lesson activity closure. While openings and closings only take a small portion of your instructional time, they need to be thoughtful when planned, as the first 10 minutes and last 10 minutes of a lesson are the most vital times for learning (Sousa, 2011). Due to a phenomenon known as the primacy-recency effect, "during a learning episode, we remember best that which comes first, second best that which comes last, and least that which comes just past the middle" (Sousa, 2011, p. 95). This reinforces the importance of strong openings and closings when designing and planning lessons.

Lesson Openings

Words to Know

Anticipatory set—an opening activity that has students engaged and in anticipation of what could be coming next

Often teachers focus so much on the actual lesson they lose the engagement, motivation, and learning that comes from developing a simple but effective lesson opening. The opening part of a lesson is often referred to by many names including: *anticipatory set, hook, advance organizer,* or even *focusing event* (Stronge & Xu, 2016). Each of these names helps to see the purpose in the opening. A good opening should have students *anticipating* what is to come next, *hook* them through engagement, and help them to *focus and organize* their thoughts. By spending time on the opening portion of your lesson, students will make a deeper connection with the content to come in the meat of the lesson. Engaging and motivating students to interact with the information will help you become an effective teacher. For more information on engaging and motivating students in the classroom, see Part 4.

Closing a Lesson

Just as opening a lesson engages students and helps prepare them to learn new information, the closing of a lesson helps students organize, evaluate, and store the information they learned (Stronge & Xu, 2016). While anticipatory sets get lots of attention and preparation by teachers, the closing is often undervalued and unplanned (Reese, 2014). While it is easy for the teacher to wrap up a lesson by pointing out what was learned, it is more powerful if students engage in the lesson closure (Pollock, 2007). The purpose in engaging students in this type of activity is three-fold:

- It provides an overview and reinforces key information.

- It assesses the level of student learning.

- It ties up loose ends and corrects misunderstandings (Finley, 2015; Stronge & Xu, 2016).

By taking a couple minutes at the end of a lesson, the teacher can quickly determine which students made a connection with the content and understood what was taught. This type of formative assessment can then help the teacher plan for future lessons and differentiate learning. Students also find the closure helpful because it allows them to do the following:

- Link new and old ideas.

- Transfer ideas to novel situations.

- Demonstrate their understanding or to clear up any misunderstandings.

- Focus on and personalize key information (Finley, 2015).

The couple of minutes at the end of a lesson can help deepen their understanding and personal connection with the material before they depart for the day or transition to another lesson.

🔧 Tools to Use

TOOL 14.1: Open with a Bang

This chart gives you options to begin a lesson that will motivate students. In addition to broader information, more specific ideas of ways to open a science lesson about the environment are suggested. The categories are the same used throughout this chapter with one exception: connecting old and new learning. While a very important category, each of the examples helps students make connections to background knowledge or information from previous lessons. These ideas can be used with a variety of grade levels, but they would need to be adjusted to meet the needs of your students.

Make It Relevant and Manageable	• Create an opening that focuses on real-world problems that students encounter. • Focus on a key question of the lesson to connect it with what comes next. • Connect new and old learning. • Show how the learning to come will affect students' personal or career goals. • Focus the opening around student interests. • Create a challenge for students that is manageable but interesting. • Use graphic organizers to organize student ideas about the upcoming topic or already known information. • As students enter the classroom, have posters or news articles spread around the room on the topic of the environment. Give students time to read an article or two and jot down a connection or question with regards to the article(s). • Read a short book or part of a book that relates to the topic of the environment. • Create a K-W-L chart with students about the environment. • Create a mind map with students about the environment.
Make It Interesting	• Pose questions or problems that are intriguing and pique students' curiosity to know more. • State facts or other interesting ideas about the concept so students want to learn more. • Use sentence strips and post seemingly unrelated words then ask students to see if they can make a connection among the words. • Use cotton balls that have been sprayed with evergreen scent to enhance the classroom. Then ask students what they smell and what connections they can make to that smell. • Have a mystery word that students have to guess.
Give Students Control	• Give students a choice in which question they answer or activity they participate in for the opening. • Give students a role in establishing rules and procedures for the upcoming activity. • Leave materials or manipulatives out for students to explore. • Allow students to choose which article to read as they enter the room. • Lay out various tools environmentalists use (or pictures of them) and let students roam the room investigating. • Ask students to choose an aspect of the environment that is important to them and write why it is important to them.

Source: Information from Akhlaq et al. (2010); McLean (2003); Stronge & Xu (2016).

TOOL 14.2: How to Deliver an Effective Introduction

The introduction is an important part of direct instruction. It is, therefore, important that the introduction is effective. Use these tips to prepare an introduction to a direct instruction lesson that will benefit your students.

Review
Start the lesson with a review of previously learned skills, homework, or prerequisite skills students will need to accomplish the target lesson. The review will informally assess students so teachers can gauge whether they are ready for the new learning or if reteaching is necessary prior to the delivery of the new lesson. List what you will review prior to the target lesson and how you will review it: ☐ Homework? ☐ Questioning so that students can recall previous learning? ☐ Prerequisite knowledge and skills needed for the new learning?
Overview
Provide an overview of the lesson. 1. Identify the goals for the lesson. _____ _____ _____ 2. Provide an outline of the lesson. _____ _____ _____ Reflections: _____ _____ _____

Source: Reprinted with permission from James Stronge (2021).

TOOL 14.3: Engaging Lesson Closings

This chart provides some interesting and engaging ways to close a lesson. There are a range of activities depending on how much time you expect to have at the end of your lesson.

3-2-1	Students list three things they learned during the lesson, two things they have questions about or wonder about, and one thing they want to tell the teacher.
Jeopardy!	Create a game of Jeopardy for students to review what was learned during the lesson.
Three Ws	*What* did we learn today? So, *what*? This speaks to relevance and connecting with students. Now *what*? This speaks to relevance in what is currently being learned in class.
Gallery Walk	Students leave their completed work in a common area and have the entire class walk around to see other's work. This is especially effective in writing and art.
Quick Doodle	Students quickly draw or doodle two or three concepts presented in the lesson. They can use numbers or words to help explain.
Quiz Creator	Students create and answer possible questions for a quiz or test. Require at least two questions to start with how or why.
Be the Teacher	Students pretend to be the teacher and teach or tell the others one thing they learned during the lesson. Each subsequent student should choose a different point.
Exit	Students complete a half sheet of paper that has one or two questions on it that reviews the concept learned in the lesson. These can be anonymous or not.
Sticky Note Round-up	Students answer a question the teacher posted in the classroom on a sticky note, and on the way out the door, they post their answer.

TOOL 14.4: Checklist for Evaluating Opening Activities

These lists can be used by teachers to examine their lesson openings to ensure they are engaging or meaningful for students. For teachers struggling to find a good opening, these questions may help you find an opening that will be relevant, interesting, or connected.

Was it relevant?

- ☐ Did it involve a real-world issue or problem?
- ☐ Did it relate to something going on in lives of the students currently?
- ☐ Did it relate to personal or life goals for students?

Was it interesting?

- ☐ Did you do something unexpected?
- ☐ Did you do something unusual or out of character?
- ☐ Did you do something creative?
- ☐ Did you do something thoughtful?
- ☐ Did you do something dramatic?

Did students have control?

- ☐ Did students have a choice in activities or questions?
- ☐ Did students get to explore materials in any way?

Did it connect to old and new learning?

- ☐ Did you make a connection between what students already know to what they will be learning?
- ☐ Did you use a graphic organizer to show the relationship between new and old knowledge?

3

15 Lesson Planning to Support Students' Individual Learning Needs

Recognizing Differences

Students from all walks of life, with differing background experiences and abilities, will populate your classroom. Recognizing these individual differences and understanding how to best develop each individual student is critical to student success. Also, recognizing the differences among individuals and groups of students and adjusting instruction to meet those differences is a quality of effective teachers (Tomlinson, 2014).

While students come to school with a great range of abilities, there are three recognized groups you may find in your classroom: general education students, gifted and talented students, and special needs students. Within each of these groups there will be a wide range of student differences, and as the teacher with an inclusive classroom, it will be your job to consider and accommodate the following:

- The individual needs of students while creating a natural learning community.

- Each student's educational needs as well as the general well-being of each student and the class as a whole.

- The fact that you must be flexible enough in implementing the curriculum to meet the individual needs of students.

- External pressures of testing and the internal pull to do what is best for the students in the class (Molbaek, 2018).

Designing Instruction for Students with Special Needs within the Curriculum

Helping students with special needs to succeed with the general education curriculum may be something you need to do and plan for as a teacher, even if you are not a teacher of students with special needs. Inclusive education continues to proliferate in schools as students are placed into the least restrictive environment to meet their individual learning needs. The individualized education plan (IEP) will address special education services and help these students access the general education curriculum. If you have students with an IEP or a Section 504 plan in your classroom, be sure you know what is written in those documents. While you are preparing your lesson plans you will need to know the accommodations for working with these students to help them be successful, which will need to be considered during the planning process. Some additional ways to help and plan for your students with special needs include the following:

- Ensure you have a structured support system, including the school leadership team, to support you and answer questions, if needed.

- Ensure your classroom is an inclusive environment where all students feel valued and important.

- Ensure you build relationships with students with special needs so that you can make decisions on the best way to teach them and so that you can anticipate any misconceptions or difficulties that may arise.

- Ensure you are sharing knowledge and seeking expertise when you need it.

- Ensure you use appropriate and evidenced-based instructional practices. If you need help finding these best practices, reach out to the special education collaborating teacher assigned to your specific student or to the leadership team within the school (Garvey et al., 2020; Mahoney, 2020).

Planning for Talented and Gifted Students

Within your classroom you may have students who have been or are in the process of being identified as gifted and talented. These students have the capability to perform at higher levels compared to others in the same peer group, experience, and environment in one or more areas of learning (National Association for Gifted Children, n.d.). Due to these capabilities, changes to instruction need to be planned in order to help them recognize and fulfill their ability. These students can come from all walks of life and need

3

 Words to Know

Inclusion—the partial or total integration of students with special needs into the age-appropriate general education classroom

Individualized Education Plan (IEP)— a document created for students with special needs that denotes the accommodations and required details for working with these students so they are able to access and succeed with the agreed-upon learning expectations

support and guidance in developing socially and emotionally as well as in their area(s) of exceptionality (NAGC, n.d.).

Characteristics of gifted students include precocity, complexity, and intensity. They can be creative, have good conceptual understanding, and exhibit some perfectionistic tendencies. While these learners have strengths, they also have weaknesses, and it is important to use their strengths to build up their weaknesses. As you plan for your gifted and talented students, be mindful to

- Ensure students are challenged in their area(s) of talent.

- Give students the capacity to be themselves and work independently.

- Provide subject and grade-level based acceleration when educational needs call for it.

- Give students the ability to socialize and work with like-ability and non-alike-ability peers.

- Differentiate both the content and the pace of instruction, as appropriate (Rogers, 2007).

Supporting Students Who Are Twice Exceptional

Words to Know

Complexity—taking an assignment and adding additional elements to require connections to be made across time, people, perspectives, or disciplines

Twice exceptional *(2e)*—students who are identified as having special needs and are also identified as gifted and talented

In addition to the students with special needs and gifted students, some students can be twice exceptional (2e). What does that mean? It means that the student has simultaneous characteristics of a student with special needs and of a gifted student. These students tend to go unnoticed as the characteristics of each may mask the other (Wiley, 2020). These 2e learners should not be confused with a gifted student who is under-achieving because there is an underlying cause for the twice exceptionality (Josephson et al., 2018). In fact, 2e students may have lower self-efficacy, motivation, and self-regulatory skills than typical gifted students, so recognizing both their giftedness and their unique needs is important. However, focusing on the gifted characteristics first then the special needs characteristics will help improve student attitudes toward school (Alotaibi, 2017; Lee & Ritchotte, 2018; McCoach et al., 2020). So how do you support and plan for 2e students in your classroom? According to Josephson et al. (2018), you should

- Ensure you focus on the strengths of the students by providing opportunities for choice and offering several ways for students to react to new material.

- Be explicit in linking prior learning to new learning.

- Help students with organizational skills when needed.

- Ensure you support students' social and emotional needs by helping them learn self-advocacy techniques as well as stress management.

- Use the school's resources, such as the school counselor, gifted education teacher, special needs education teacher, or your administration to help by offering support or ideas to better meet the learning needs of these students.

- Build a relationship with the student's outside support system, family, therapists, and tutors (get signed permission from guardians prior to working with others; most districts have a consent to exchange information form to be completed) to share strategies that have worked for them and to help get a more full picture of the student.

- Create lessons that can offer both challenge and remediation.

How many 2e students are in our schools? It depends on the school district but looking nationwide only 3 percent of gifted and talented students have been identified as having special needs (Harwin, 2019). This is just a small fraction of the 14 percent of students identified as special needs, yet the phenomenon is becoming more common as screening practices shift. Therefore, as a new teacher it is important to understand a 2e child might be sitting in your classroom needing help as their giftedness masks their disability.

⚒ Tools to Use

TOOL 15.1: Ways to Adapt Instruction for Learners with Special Needs

Depending on a student's individualized education plan (IEP), teachers may need to differentiate or add support for students with special needs in a variety of ways within the classroom. The case manager assigned to the student can help you find the best way to meet their needs. In addition, the following chart lists ways you can support and plan for all students in your classroom whether they are students with special needs, gifted students, or general education students. Different learners will need varying levels of support and implementation, which is why getting to know your students and then addressing their unique needs is so important! This checklist will help you take stock of some ways you can plan to adapt your instruction for learners with special needs.

	I don't do this	I need to improve on this	Good	Excellent
Assessments				
I plan for and use a diverse array of assessments as opposed to only pencil/paper assessments.				
I provide models or examples for students so that they know the expectation.				
I use formative assessments to monitor student progress.				
I plan in order to give each student an appropriate amount of time to complete an assignment or assessment.				
Collaborative Learning				
I allow students to work together in order to give everyone a chance to see various learning strategies and ways of thinking.				
Students have assigned roles during collaborative learning so I can gauge their contributions to group work.				
Explicit Instruction				
I plan to use explicit instruction when a student is struggling with a concept.				
I work with the special education teacher to alter the content or delivery when needed.				
I have broken down assignments in a step-by-step manner during planning to help students see the big picture of what needs to be done and how to get there during instruction.				
I choose my examples during planning and instruction carefully so as not to confuse students.				
I plan and teach concepts and processes in chunks as opposed to all at once.				
I organize the information students need to learn before teaching it.				

	I don't do this	I need to improve on this	Good	Excellent
Feedback				
I plan to give students feedback at multiple points during an assignment to help them reflect on their work and take note of what is going well and what needs to be changed.				
I use guided practice as a way to deliver feedback immediately to clear up any errors in student understanding.				
Graphic Organizers				
I use graphic organizers to help students see the information in an orderly and visual manner.				
I use graphic organizers to help students develop meaningful patterns of information.				
I use graphic organizers to help students chunk information.				
Modify Directions				
I plan modified instructions to prevent any misunderstandings.				
My directions give a clear idea of what needs to be accomplished and the resources available.				
Multisensory Approach				
I plan to use multiple senses to teach new concepts.				
I give students multiple ways and opportunities to interact with new concepts.				
Linking Prior Knowledge				
I build on students' prior knowledge and background experiences.				
I link new information to previously learned concepts to help student memory and recall.				
I use cues to help students transfer previously learned information.				

Source: Information from Nolet & McLaughlin (2005).

3

TOOL 15.2: Ways to Differentiate Assignments for Gifted Students

Students who identify as gifted and talented may need to have assignments and assessments altered to add complexity and depth. In order to accomplish this, the teacher needs to examine the original planned assessment and differentiate it to add either complexity or depth. Additionally, if the assignment is differentiated, then the way the assignment is assessed will need to be differentiated to address the added elements. In these examples, a teacher may provide multiple rubrics for students answering different questions.

Assignment	Add Complexity	Add Depth
After reading *The Odyssey*, write an essay explaining Odysseus's point of view.	After reading *The Odyssey*, write an essay comparing and contrasting two different characters' points of view.	After reading *The Odyssey*, write an essay explaining Odysseus's point of view and justify his actions based on his point of view.
Based on your knowledge of animal adaptations, describe the adaptations of three different animals.	Based on your knowledge of animal adaptations, describe the adaptations of three animals within a single ecosystem and determine how these adaptations impact the ecosystem.	Based on your knowledge of animal adaptations, evaluate the impact of human activity on an ecosystem.

Words to Know

Depth—taking an assignment and adjusting it so that students must show a higher level of understanding of the content or subject matter

TOOL 15.3: Twice Exceptional Student Scenario

The following scenario is an example of a twice exceptional student in the 1st grade.

A student in your classroom, Owen, is very bright. He is precocious and has a deep interest in engineering. In fact, he wants to know how everything works! He reads books about how things work and is able to apply the information he reads to new situations and in a unique manner. Often, he will link information from one subject to the next and picks up on new material quickly. He reads three grade levels above his current grade level and helps his classmates when needed. However, when it comes to writing, Owen struggles. The writing he produces is marginally grade level work, but his spelling is an even bigger concern. While Owen has passed all his spelling tests and his phonemic awareness assessments, when it comes to spelling in his writing assignments, he often shows a lack of phonological awareness and frequently misspells words that he has gotten correct on his spelling tests. As you talk with Owen about his writing, it is apparent he knows what he wants to communicate, but he has a hard time retrieving the words he wants; instead, he often uses the term "thing" when he gets tired of trying to retrieve the specific noun he wants. When asked about the "thing," he is able to describe what it looks like and how it works, but the word just escapes him. During writing, Owen puts forth a lot of effort and often breaks down in frustration as he can't think of words and when he can, he has trouble figuring out how to spell the words, and when he finally gets it down, the vowel sound and what is written are not usually aligned. On his report card, Owen continues to perform above grade level, but something seems off.

Owen's parents decide to have him educationally tested, and he falls within the 99th percentile for intellect, but he is also shown to have an expressive language disorder and dyslexia.

What are some accommodations you can use and plan to use in order to help Owen in the classroom?

- ☐ Plan more complex assignments or assignments with more depth in areas of strength to meet his gifted needs.
- ☐ Give extended time on writing assignments.
- ☐ Plan for a structured and multi-sensory phonics approach with him in small group.
- ☐ Use a word bank on written assignments
- ☐ Plan to pair auditory information with visual cues.
- ☐ Allow for written work to be dictated or use assistive technology, such as a speech-to-text program, for writing assignments.
- ☐ Give extra time for oral responses in class.
- ☐ Provide a safe space for him to regroup when/if he gets frustrated during writing.
- ☐ Provide ways for him to get positive feedback and recognition on areas of strength.

Can you think of other accommodations or modifications to the general curriculum that might help? How does having a student such as Owen change your general classroom plan?

3

Planning for and Supporting ELL Students

Growth of English Language Learners in Our Schools

English language learners (ELLs) are the fastest growing student population making its way into the general classroom setting. In the fall of 2018, ELL students accounted for 10.2 percent of students in the public school system, or roughly 5 million students (NCES, 2021). In addition to continued growth throughout the United States, individual states are growing even more significantly in their populations of ELL students. In fact, 10 states have more than 10 percent of their student population who are ELLs, and 23 states have a population between 6 and 10 percent (NCES, 2021).

Given their cultural and language diversity, educating this group of students remains a challenge. On average, it takes an ELL student between four and seven years to become academically English proficient (Weyer, 2018). In addition, ELL students often struggle academically when compared with their non-ELL peers. On a recent National Assessment of Educational Progress (NAEP) assessment, they found that 14 percent of ELL students scored at the proficient or above level in math while 40 percent of their non-ELL peers scored at the proficient or above level (Weyer, 2018). In reading, the statistics are similar with 9 percent of ELL students scoring proficient or above and 40 percent of non-ELL students performing at the proficient or above level (Weyer, 2018). This achievement gap is typically greater when ELL students begin school, and the gap often closes slowly if at all (Soland & Sandilos, 2021). This difficulty in achievement is partially responsible for a higher dropout rate and lower college attendance of ELL students when compared to their non-ELL peers (Callahan, 2013; Kanno & Cromley, 2013).

Students who are receiving ELL services face unique challenges in the classroom because they are learning a new language in addition to the content and skills that their peers are learning. Many schools and school districts serve these students through ELL programs that either "pull out" or "push in" to the general education classroom for a few hours of ELL services a week (Guler, 2020). Thus, the general education teacher plays a vital role in the success of ELL students as they spend most of their time in the mainstream classroom (Guler, 2020).

Classifying English Language Learners

While it is apparent that ELL students are a growing population and can face unique challenges, as a teacher who will most likely have ELL students in your classroom—if not now, then later—it is important to understand how the students' English proficiencies are classified and what these classifications mean for students. According to the Teachers of English Speakers of Other Languages (TESOL) International Association (2006), there are five levels of language proficiency:

1. Starting (L1): Students at this level have little or no understanding of English and rarely use it in their day-to-day lives. These students will respond to simple commands and statements using nonverbal actions or ways to express themselves. Students often use graphics to construct meaning from a text.
2. Emerging (L2): Students have graduated to using short sentences and phrases and have limited communication skills, which is usually focused on routine items or everyday words.
3. Developing (L3): Students at level 3 understand more complex speech but still may require repetition when being spoken to. These students spontaneously use their English but continue to have difficulty expressing all the ideas they have due to a limited vocabulary and/or language structure.
4. Expanding (L4): Students have language skills that are adequate for most of their daily communication, and they are able to use English in new and unfamiliar settings but may have difficulty with abstract ideas or concepts as well as complex language structures.
5. Bridging (L5): Students have the ability to express themselves with fluency and spontaneity across a broad range of topics, including academic, personal, and social. These students are on the verge of being functional with non-ELL peers with little to no support.

In addition to these levels and as a result of the Every Student Succeeds Act (ESSA) signed into law in 2015, each state must also plan and demonstrate that it has adopted English language proficiency standards (U.S. Department of Education, 2015). These standards are separate from the Common Core Standards or other standards a state has put into place. As a result, there are different organizations that have developed standards for ELL students and attempted to align them with content standards, which can be challenging (Lee, 2018). The ELL teacher assigned to support the students in the class will have assessed the ELL students as far as their level of proficiency and will be working toward achieving these standards. Knowing your student's proficiency level and what language goals they are working toward will help you better meet their needs when planning for instruction.

Tools to Use

TOOL 16.1: Planning Considerations for ELL Students

When planning for best practice, the teacher's goal is to meet all students' instructional needs. This does not require us to develop a plan for each student, but when developing instructional plans, you do need to consider what instructional materials, strategies, and resources are a best fit. This can be a challenge, but it is important when you are planning to take the time to think about what support techniques you can put into place for your ELL students. Getting feedback from the ELL teacher on various instructional strategy choices, as well as what supports would align with the needs of the ELL level, will help you to meet the needs of your ELL learners. This list of considerations when planning for the ELL students in your class can help you keep in mind their challenges of learning a new language as well as the content and skills you teach.

Resource Considerations	Instructional Considerations	Support Needed
• How can I encourage fruitful discussions among my students? • What resources can I incorporate that might be helpful to my ELL students?	• How can I scaffold this concept or skill? • What visuals, graphic organizers, and/or labels for diagrams are important? • How can I show the skills or concepts and not just talk about them? • How can I provide the students time to discuss and explain their understanding of the skills or content taught?	• Can I work with the ELL teacher to plan the lesson and follow up? • Can I work with the ELL teacher to help assess my ELL students?

TOOL 16.2: Worksheet for Meeting with the ELL Teacher or Specialist

Ensuring that you understand how to best support these students while they are under your tutelage in the classroom is something the ELL teacher/specialist can assist you with. Using collaborative planning with the ELL teacher/specialist can provide insight to instructional strategies, as well as resources, to use (Porter, 2018). This worksheet can help when you meet with the ELL teacher/specialist to discuss your ELL students as you address the unique needs of this population.

Who are my ELL students?
Do we have a set of ELL standards that our school/district uses?
What are my ELL students' language proficiency levels?
What are my ELL students able to do at their given levels when considering my lesson plans?
What instructional strategies can I use to help my ELL students to better understand the content and the skills being taught while also helping them increase their English vocabulary and language skills?
What miscues or misunderstandings specifically related to language should I look for during the lesson for these students?

3

17 Integrating Technology into Lesson Plans to Advance Student Learning

The Technology Possibilities

Technological advances in the past two decades have ushered in enormous capabilities to enhance learning, but they also have the capability to take the place of learning. It is up to you, the teacher, to ensure that technology is integrated into your classroom so that it supports your work—and your students. From research we know that there is a link between student engagement and achievement in the classroom, so understanding how technology influences student engagement is important and can inform your teaching practice (Schuetz et al., 2018). Using technology in the classroom opens many possibilities for your students to interact with content, people, and places never thought possible a few years ago. However, if students are not provided sufficient guidance and modeling in how to use technological tools in the classroom to enhance their learning, these learning benefits don't accrue (Barak, 2017). So when planning lessons, the potential that technology provides must be considered within the constructs of what we know about good teaching and learning to help guide the best implementation in the classroom (Greene et al., 2018).

> **🔤 Words to Know**
>
> *Integration*—acting to unite different things, in this case technology and teaching/learning

Integrating Technology into Your Classroom

If you were to ask a random sample of teachers what technology integration looks like, the answer would range between using a PowerPoint presentation, to having students blog, to having students create computer code. The question then becomes, are all these teachers integrating technology into their classrooms most productively? And the answer may be yes but at different levels and depending on the teaching circumstances. Puentedura (2013) created a model for technology integration that is similar to how you might use Bloom's taxonomy to determine cognitive depth of learning. The model can help you determine how comfortable you are with technology integration and what the next steps can be to further enhance technology integration in the classroom. The model is called the SAMR (substitution, augmentation, modification, redefinition). Within the model technology can be a *substitution* for a task or product and changes it little. Technology can *augment* the lesson where it acts as a substitute but allows for more functionality than just a replacement. In *modification*, technology allows for significant change in the design of a task or product, and in *redefinition* the technology allows for the creation of a new task. Technology can be used in a variety of ways within the classroom with substitution and augmentation enhancing the classroom, and modification and redefinition transforming the classroom. This is not to say that every lesson should be at the redefine stage of integration, as that would not be prudent, but it can help you gauge where you are in your technology integration and see how to move from enhancement to transformation if that is your goal. To see possible ways to use these levels in the classroom, please see the tools in this chapter.

Technology Integration Attributes

While it is great to know about the technology available to you, integrating available technology in a manner that is consistent with best practices calls for teachers to shift their behaviors and their mindsets. For example, if you use technology prominently in your instructional delivery, you must be flexible enough to pivot when things go haywire, because with newer technologies they often will. The following list of attributes describe how teachers and students must respond to allow for the integration of technology:

1. **Being adaptable and comfortable with changing situations.** Technology is always changing, and to keep up students and teachers must be able to adapt. Additionally, technology often does not behave the way we anticipate, so there needs to be some comfort in pivoting when something goes awry.

2. **Collaborating and communicating in an environment that is not confined within the classroom walls.** Teachers must be comfortable with students working together and with others outside the classroom space. This feeling might be a bit unsettling, as the teacher does not necessarily have control over the space.

3. **Creating and organizing data and information.** As technology changes, it affects the amount of information available, and students and teachers need to be able to manage the influx of information and organize it in a meaningful way. This also means being able to share the information in a way that keeps up with the technology train.

4. **Relenting control.** Similar to giving up the control of the classroom space, you may have to change your thinking about control. While you still retain control over the content and pedagogy, you must relent some control over product and process to the students (Barak, 2017).

🔧 Tools to Use

TOOL 17.1: How Technology Enhances Teaching and Learning

As noted earlier, technology can enhance teaching and learning when used in conjunction with what we already know is good teaching practice to ensure learning. So, what are some ways that technology can enhance your teaching or your students' learning? This chart looks in-depth at key aspects of teaching and learning that can be enhanced with technology and how they can be applied to the classroom. While only a couple of examples are listed, there are numerous ways technology can be integrated. However you choose to integrate technology in your classroom, it is important to ensure you are using best practices and not just technology for technology's sake.

3

🔤 Words to Know

Trace data—a digital record created when students use features provided by technology (Bernacki et al., 2020)

	Impact on Students	Impact on Teachers	Possible Tools
Access	• Students can see content in new and different ways, and they can reach out to or read material by experts in the field. • Special education students have the ability to access the regular curriculum.	• Teachers can give extra help to students who may need it or enrich students who need the challenge. • Teachers can use assistive technology to allow students with special needs to access the curriculum.	• Use voice to text. • Use translation software for families or ESL students. • Use software for visually impaired or hearing impaired. • Use technology to visit museums or attend virtual field trips.
Accommodations	Students can be given assignments that are personalized to their learning level.	• Teachers can use student trace data, or the digital record or footprint left when information is changed, to adjust instruction. • Teachers can help students with special needs by personalizing their learning.	• Have students record and present on a device instead of live. • Use discussion boards as opposed to in person participation. • Have students record themselves reading a book.
Assessment	• Students can participate in assessments that adapt to their readiness level. • Students can work at their own speed and pace themselves.	Teachers can use trace data and see the process students used in real time to see how they got to their product.	Use computer adaptive tests.

	Impact on Students	Impact on Teachers	Possible Tools
Collaboration	• Students can create content with peers. • Students can interact with content via technology as well as consume, edit, or create without constriction of space and time.	• Using technology allows teachers to connect with others outside the classroom to enhance practice. • There are few limitations on space or time for collaborating.	• Use Google docs so students can collaborate on work. • Use wikis or blogs to enable multiple students to participate.
Communication	Students can connect with others, allowing them to have access to peers, educators, and experts around the world.	• Teachers can connect and collaborate with each other and experts without having to hold an in-person meeting. • Teachers can share information and student work with parents digitally.	• Create a class website for parents and students. • Use Skype, Google Meet, Zoom, or other meeting platforms.
Creativity	Students can create different products using different forms of technology based on the same learning objectives or standards.	• Teachers can promote creativity with students by using a variety of technology to teach and give assignments. • Teachers can use technology to enhance the creativity of the lesson.	Use a variety of multimedia tools with students or allow students to use these tools to create products.
Feedback	Students can receive prompt feedback from a computer program or the teacher.	Teachers can provide immediate feedback to students.	• Use trace data to give students feedback on their thinking and methods. • Use the feedback from computer adaptive tests to review student results. • Use Kahoot! or some other question game that gives students immediate feedback. • Peer feedback can be provided using Google docs or similar technology.

3

Words to Know

Web quest—an activity where students are given a task to complete and use the online resources to complete it

	Impact on Students	Impact on Teachers	Possible Tools
Exploration	Students can explore different topics and ideas based on personal preference using differing modalities.	Teachers can explore content to be taught at a different depth and include more information in lessons.	• Use web quests, activities where students are given a task and use online resources to complete it, to give students a safe way to explore an idea or topic online. • Create a document with various resource links that students can access to explore content or new ideas.
Research	Students can use technology to conduct research to expand their learning and understanding of a concept or idea.	Teachers can use technology to teach students how to research and be good consumers of research and good digital citizens.	• Use various sources on the web to teach students how to be consumers of research. • Teach lessons about how to create passwords to protect themselves and their content as well as how to interact politely and safely to show examples and nonexamples.

TOOL 17.2: The SAMR Model in the Classroom

This tool offers a more in-depth look at how technology can be integrated. It also shows how you can move from enhancing the classroom with technology to transforming it (Puentedura, 2013). The simple definition for each level is included as well as an example of what this might look like in the classroom.

Redefine	Technology allows for the creation of a new task.	Example: Have students create a blog on a given topic in which they collaborate with others in their group using a Google document. Students enhance their blog by creating videos, podcasts, and interviews with experts on the topic.
Modify	Technology allows for a significant change in the design of the task or product.	Example: Have students create a blog where they type their papers and information in a Google document. Groups of students can collaborate to produce and publish the blog.
Augment	Technology acts as a substitute for the task or product that allows for more functionality.	Example: Have students type their paper into a Google doc, which is then commented on by other students in the class.
Substitute	Technology acts as a substitute for the task or product that changes it little.	Example: Have students type a paper into a Google doc instead of writing it on pencil and paper.

TOOL 17.3: Lesson Plan Integrating Technology

This lesson plan for 2nd or 3rd grade students is an example of how to use technology to augment student learning. The technology allows for students to run a lemonade stand and make decisions for their business. Setting up a lemonade stand at the school would be a challenge, but the technology allows for the activity. It augments the lesson! Additionally, using the Google Sheet allows the teacher to ask questions and get formative assessment in real time and interact with the students as they manipulate the recipe and the amount of goods they purchase.

Teacher: Mr. Chang

Date: March 3

Subject/Content: Social Studies/Economics

Standard(s) Addressed: This section of the template helps you plan what the students should know at the end of the lesson.

- CA2.4—Students understand and can demonstrate basic economic reasoning.
- CA2.4.2/2.4.3—Students understand the role and interdependence of consumers and producers of goods and services.

Students understand how limited resources impacts production and consumption.

(California Department of Education, 2000)

Materials: List your materials or resources here, so you know you have everything needed for the lesson.

- *Prices! Prices! Prices!: Why They Go Up and Down* book
- Computers for each grouping of students
- Google Sheet with heading for data collection (temp outside, amount of goods bought, sales for the day, goods that went to waste)

Reference: Adler, D. A. (2016) *Prices! Prices! Prices!: Why they go up and down.* Holiday House.

Stage 1: Introduction (Orientation) – Gains student attention; clarifies learning objectives and student expectations

Anticipatory Set: THE HOOK – Strategies to motivate students to engage in this lesson including activating prior knowledge

- The class will create a KWL chart about consumers and producers and the cost of goods.
- Read the book *Prices! Prices! Prices!: Why They Go Up and Down* to students, stopping every so often to ask questions. The class will add new information to the KWL.

Learning Objective: As a result of this lesson students will demonstrate their knowledge of ＿＿＿＿＿ basic economics ＿＿＿＿＿ in the following way(s):

Students will be able to explain why prices of goods (lemonade) might change.

Students will be able to explain why resources impact the amount of goods (lemonade) made and sold.

Students will make decisions for their lemonade stand based on a set of conditions and explain why they made the decisions they did for their stand.

Lesson Intention: Articulating the learning intention from the student's perspective: student-friendly language, including purpose and/or connection to the real world. Students need to know what is expected of them. The intentions can be stated and if required by your school written daily in the classroom.

Today I will learn… how and why economic decisions are made.

I can… make economic decisions for my lemonade stand based on a set of conditions and/or criteria.

This is important because… it shows the impact of my decisions on the amount of resources and how that impacts the amount of lemonade I can make and the amount of lemonade I can sell within the simulation.

Stage 2: Main Lesson Presentation – Explains the new content or demonstrates a new task or concept; this is what we traditionally think of as "teaching"

Task(s)	Description
Model Procedures Using Appropriate Instructional Strategies	• The teacher will go over with students the new vocabulary and introduce the project which will require students to think about economic principals to be successful. The students will be using the Lemonade Stand Simulation to simulate running a lemonade stand business. • The teacher goes over the important aspects of the game with students—choosing how to spend their money on lemons, ice, cups, and sugar. Also discussing with students choosing how to set a price and determining how much lemon/ice/sugar in their lemonade recipe.
Provide Examples	• The teacher will run one day of her simulation and fill in a Google sheet to keep the data. • The students will ask questions or make observations from the teacher's simulation.

Stage 3: Practice – Uses gradual release of teacher control as students transition from guided practice to independent practice; checks for understanding and provides feedback

Guided Practice, Formative Assessment and Feedback	Activity(ies)	Questions to be asked during this activity
	Students will work in small group, pairs, or individually; the teacher will have students run one day of simulation and stop to have teacher check their progress before continuing to next days.	• What decisions are you making and how is it affecting your lemonade sales? • If you change your inputs for your resources how do you think it will impact your sales?
Independent Practice	Students will work individually, in pairs, or in small groups of three to run their lemonade stand for 30 days a month.	• Which resources are most vital to protect? • How does the weather impact your decisions? • Why did you choose these inputs?
Lesson Summary and Closure	Students will determine how much money they made over the course of 30 days in their lemonade stand simulation. The students will complete a sticky note explaining which day they thought was their best and why they think that day was their bestselling day. The sticky notes will be posted on a board on the way out of class.	

3

	Activity(ies)	Questions to be asked during this activity
Assessment of performance, Opportunities for retention and transfer of learning to novel tasks	• The teacher will develop questions based on the decisions made and put into the Google Sheet. • Formative assessment.	
Other Considerations – Things to think about as you plan your lesson		
Homework Students will have a discussion at home with their parents about prices at the grocery store on certain items.		

Source: Reprinted with permission from James Stronge (2021).

3

Planning for Differentiated Instruction in Your Classroom

Why Use Differentiated Instruction?

With the continued rise of globalization and as student diversity continues to increase in many forms, we can readily see that our classrooms are a microcosm of an increasingly diverse society. Students come to your classroom from a variety of backgrounds and needs specific to who they are as individuals and as learners. To even start to successfully address the diverse learning needs of all our students, we must embrace differentiated instruction as standard practice. And the reason for differentiated instruction? It affects students in a positive way by

- Increasing student engagement, interest, and satisfaction (this is also true for teachers).

- Motivating students and causing them to be enthusiastic learners.

- Maximizing student potential.

- Encouraging student persistence.

- Increasing self-confidence in students.

- Improving students' self-directedness and metacognitive awareness.

- Producing higher academic scores for students (Suprayogi et al., 2017).

> **Words to Know**
>
> **Differentiated instruction**—"a research-based model of classroom practice intended to support teachers in developing curriculum and instruction likely to maximize the capacity of a diverse group of learners" (Tomlinson, 2015, p. 203)
>
> **Pedagogy**—the method or practice of teaching

Principles of Differentiated Instruction

Differentiated instruction values the individual when looking at teaching and learning. The following principles are key principles, attitudes, and beliefs of those committed to implementing differentiated instruction:

1. **Recognize that difference among humans is normal and desirable.** Enrichment is gained by varied perspectives from a range of learners.
2. **Think flexibly to allow for equity to access quality learning opportunities.** Understanding that just because some students need different strategies to be successful does not mean they should not receive the same quality learning experience as other students.
3. **Understand that students come to lessons and learning experiences from different places and will continue through each at different paces.** Individuals have various interests and understandings of the world around them as well as different ways to make sense of new information, so for each lesson students may have a diverse array of needs.
4. **Realize the importance of curriculum and instruction that is rigorous and relevant.** This allows for an understanding of the key concepts and ideas.
5. **Become a student for understanding your students.** This allows for knowledge on how best to engage, motivate, and teach each student. It helps when trying to determine how best to meet student needs.
6. **Reflect back on students' practice in order to adjust instruction to meet student and content needs.** This allows for ongoing assessment, not only of students and where they are in their learning, but also, of yourself to ensure activities are equally interesting and relevant to students (Kaur, 2017; Tomlinson, 2015; Tomlinson, 2017).

Stages of Differentiated Instruction

Knowing you have a diverse group of students and ensuring their needs are met are two different things. So where do you begin when planning differentiated instruction? Carol Ann Tomlinson, who was one of the first educational researchers to popularize the term *differentiated instruction* (Breen, 2019), identifies four classroom elements where teachers can differentiate based on student readiness, interest, or learning profile (Tomlinson, 2017):

1. Content—the information students need to know or how they access this information
2. Process—the way in which students interact with the content to master it
3. Product—the final way in which students show what they have learned
4. Environment—the way the classroom works, is situated, or feels

The first thing to understand about planning for differentiation is that differentiation within a lesson cannot be separated from differentiated planning and assessment (van Geel et al., 2019). Knowing the planning-instruction-assessment connection will help you look more clearly at the various stages of implementing differentiated instruction. When thinking about teaching for differentiated student needs, it makes sense that you go through the planning stages in order: (1) unit planning, (2) lesson planning, (3) instruction, and (4) assessment. However, to properly meet the needs of your diverse learners, these stages may shift. As part of the planning-instruction-assessment process for differentiation, you will base a lesson where you set goals and determine your pedagogical approach and then prepare for a matching type of evaluation (van Geel et al., 2019). Figure 18.1 gives a good visual to describe this understanding in combination with where you can differentiate during these stages.

FIGURE 18.1 Stages of Differentiated Instruction

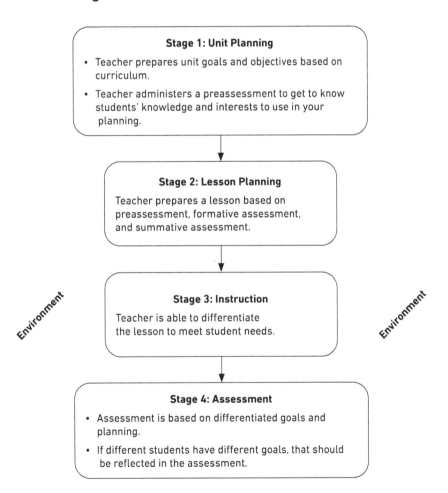

Source: Information from Tomlinson (2017) and van Geel et al. (2019).

Looking at the shift in stages, it is important to first know your students and how they are performing academically related to the goals/objectives you will be teaching.

As you plan out your unit of study and set goals, use feedback from preassessments and your knowledge of students to differentiate. Next, when you are preparing lessons within the unit, you can differentiate the process, set whole-group objectives, and then set small-group objectives that still align with the overarching goals. As the lesson is taking place, monitor students and use formative feedback to continually adapt to meet students' needs. If a student needs extra help, create an opportunity to reteach or an activity to help build understanding differently. Lastly, when you assess students, there is another opportunity to differentiate. Students can create different products or have different assessment questions based on the instructional process taken.

🔧 Tools to Use

TOOL 18.1: How to Make Differentiated Instruction Work in Your Classroom

While the stages of how to plan for differentiated instruction are helpful in showing how planning, assessment, and instruction are intertwined, knowing within those categories where and how you can diversify is important. Using a preassessment tool helps you gauge your students' knowledge and interests in the upcoming learning. Do you have to diversify every aspect of every lesson? No! Start small and build. Choose one aspect of your instruction to differentiate; then, as that becomes familiar with how to differentiate your instruction, add another. This incremental approach to learning and using effective differentiated instructional practices will help you feel confident in your abilities to actually differentiate instruction.

Preassessment
Why? 1. As much as we try to be students of our students, we cannot know everything about what they know and understand. 2. This can help plan for differentiation of content, process, product, and environment.

Classroom of Diverse Learners
How? • Academics • Culture • Language • Gender • Experience • Ability • Learning style • Personal interests • Economics • Motivation • Social-emotional

Differentiate How?

3

Teacher
As the teacher, you cannot control the diversity of your students, but you can plan for it! Using information from the preassessment and knowledge of your students you can impact the content, process, product, and environment to help meet student's diverse needs.

Content	Process	Product	Environment
• Adjust reading materials. • Allow for different modes for accessing content such as visual or auditory. • Create small flexible groups. • Reteach. • Use different vocabulary lists. • Curriculum compact. • Use different levels of questioning.	• Design tiered activities based on preassessment. • Vary the pace. • Provide different levels of hands-on support. • Alter the depth or complexity of study on the topic.	Give choice of product. For example: • Write a journal or record thoughts on a video or on a podcast. • Create posters, presentations, or Power-point presentations. • Put on a play, write an essay, or create a comic strip.	• Include quiet areas. • Include areas where groups can work together. • Have different types of seating such as yoga balls, chairs, or standing desks. • Ensure classroom management supports a safe, inviting, and supportive learning space.

Source: Information from Johnsen (2017); Kaur (2017); van Geel et al. (2019).

TOOL 18.2: Differentiation Self-Assessment

This tool can be used as a teacher self-assessment to determine if you are helping ensure differentiated instruction will be successful in your classroom. These questions can help you reflect on your planning, instruction, assessment, and environment to see if you are meeting all your students' needs.

		What changes can I make?
Relationship to Students	☐ Do I show an interest in my students as individuals and not just academically? ☐ Do I believe that each student has the capacity to succeed academically? How do I convey this to the students?	
Content	☐ Am I using small groups? ☐ Am I using different levels of questioning? ☐ Am I diversifying the materials available, both within and outside the curriculum? ☐ Do I provide opportunities for students to use different modalities to access the curriculum? ☐ Do I use flexible grouping? ☐ Do I understand the content deeply enough to structure it differently for different learners? ☐ Do I plan proactively? ☐ Have I made it a point to ensure students know the key learning targets?	
Process	☐ Do I build on students' existing knowledge, skills, and attitudes? ☐ Do I use a variety of activities? ☐ Do students have different ways to get to the same end point?	
Products	☐ Do I allow students to choose how to display their knowledge? ☐ Do I provide various ways and assessments for students to show their understanding? ☐ Do I use the information collected from assessment to differentiate my instruction?	
Environment	☐ Do I have routines in place for students to follow when I'm not available to help? ☐ Do I have a variety of materials out and available to students for use? ☐ Did I go over expectations for behavior with students? ☐ Do I have a variety of places around my classroom where students can work independently, in a group, quietly, or in discussion? ☐ Is my classroom student-centered? ☐ Have I set up a classroom where it is OK to take risks and fail in order to succeed?	

Source: Information from Smets (2017) and Tomlinson (2015).

TOOL 18.3: Differentiated Project Plan

This tool provides a differentiated project plan for middle school students who are learning about the westward expansion of the United States. As you review this project plan, note that it is differentiated by product (students choose how to create their commercial) and process (students determine their role in the group). The students were assessed using a rubric.

Changing Mindsets: Westward Expansion Project

Driving Question: How did inventions and adaptations of the 19th century revolutionize the Wild West?

Task: You are an advertising executive who has to sell a new invention. Create an advertisement that convinces Western settlers/farmers/ranchers that your invention/adaptation will revolutionize, or at least improve, their lives.

Indicator 2.a.3 Essential: Identify the following inventions and explain how people used them to adapt to life in challenging environments:

- Barbed wire/steel plows/dry farming/sod houses/beef cattle raising/wheat farming/windmills/railroads

Expectations: Students should create a professional-looking advertisement (no more than three minutes long) to persuade Western settlers, ranchers, and/or cowboys that your assigned technology will revolutionize or improve their lives in the Wild West.

At the end of each presentation, groups are expected to be able to answer questions about the project. Make sure that your group is prepared and ready with background knowledge. You must understand the following questions:

- What did the technology do?

- How did it shape/change life in the West?

- Where and when would it have been used?

- Who would have used it?

Every member of the group is expected to contribute equally, and at the end of the project, students will report on their work.

3

Presentation Suggestions: Students will create an advertisement. This can be done using technology to create a video, acting out a "live commercial," creating a pamphlet, or any other idea appropriate method (just have your group get the idea approved by the teacher first). They will be required to present their advertisement to the class.

Group Roles: All group members should work together and help each other—even if the task falls outside of their job description!

- **Pioneer:** group leader, responsible for checking in with everyone, making sure everyone is on task and on schedule, making sure the research and presentation is focused on the driving question, and making sure your group understands and follows the rubric.

- **Miner:** lead researcher

- **Cowboy/cowgirl:** responsible for production and creation of the advertisement (including writing a script, creating the video, and other details including editing the presentation)

- **Mercantile manager:** get necessary supplies and materials for the team and make sure that the team has cleaned up its area at the end of the day. Be sure you keep written documentation of all activities and help prepare digital/print materials. Also, seek input from each person and, if necessary, call the teacher over to ask a team question.

Source: Reprinted with permission from Isoldi (2021).

TOOL 18.4: Differentiated Project Plan Worksheet

Use this template to help plan your differentiated project or lesson. Make sure you remember to include the roles and an explanation of each role. Include resources students can use to help them complete the task and take into consideration the timeline for the project. Before starting, make sure you know where you want your students to end up.

Project Title:	
Class:	
Driving Question:	
Task:	
Timeline:	
Learning Objectives:	**Essential Questions:**
Expectations:	**Presentation Suggestions for Students:**
Resources for Students to Use:	
Groups and Roles:	

3

19 Planning Collaboratively

The Benefits of Collaborative Planning

Teacher collaboration usually refers to a way in which teachers work together to combine their resources to achieve specific goals, such as students' learning, over a set time period (Vangrieken et al., 2015). While this concept of working together seems quite simple, in a profession that is often characterized by isolation, it can be challenging. The term *collaboration* differs from cooperation in the sense that collaborating requires the group assembled to "explore complex problems, develop deeper understandings of the challenges and opportunities the problems present, and work to develop thoughtful solutions" (Herrmann, 2019, p. 70). Planning, which is a complex compilation of understanding curriculum, instruction, and assessment (CIA), is the perfect place for teachers to collaborate. When collaboration is paired with planning, many benefits arise. In fact, the following lists show the benefits of collaborative planning at many different levels within the school:

Personal benefits:

- On the job professional development

- Proactive search for self-learning

- Builds self-confidence in subject matter and teaching ability

- Gain new ideas and current materials

- Increases knowledge on how to reach diverse student populations

- Encourages trying new things in the classroom and taking risks

Interpersonal benefits:

- Cultivates trust and openness

- Gives members of the team the ability to be reflective

- Counters a culture of individual isolation

- Fosters a sense of sharing among subjects, grade levels, and other areas (special education, gifted education, ELL, etc.)

Schoolwide benefits:

- Helps teachers build and enhance support networks within the school building

- Shows learner-centric culture of support

- Supports professional dialogue

- Supports advanced planning

- Allows teachers to lead initiatives (Hargreaves, 2019; Nguyen & Ng, 2020; Stronge & Xu, 2016; Tóth Pjeczka et al., 2019)

In addition to having these benefits for teachers and the school, collaboration can improve the quality of lesson plans. When teachers work collaboratively on lesson plans, improvements can be seen in all aspects—from the selecting of learning objectives for students to developing instructional steps to the use of materials and media for the lesson and assessment (Stronge & Xu, 2016). Importantly, collaborative lesson planning also benefits students. By collaborating, teachers and others can share information regarding student needs, knowledge, interests, and experiences, as well as help each other develop plans to accommodate developmental and individual differences, including culturally responsive teaching practices (Stronge & Xu, 2016).

Collaborative Planning: How to Do It

When you first start collaborative planning, it might feel a bit overwhelming, but once it becomes a regular part of your routine, it will become a vital part of your schedule! Most collaborative teams have a facilitator—this can be the team leader as identified by the school, a group leader agreed upon by those in the planning session, or even an administrator. The facilitator's job is to define the purpose and expectations of the collaborative sessions as well as keep the team focused (Stronge & Xu, 2016). Likewise, it is the responsibility of all group members to make sure they are focusing on improving their teaching skills through discussion specific to instruction and strategies used, as well as setting goals for the team (Stronge & Xu, 2016). In order for these collaborative planning sessions to be useful to you, it is important that all members recognize the

3

group is mutually dependent, collectively responsible, jointly open to new ideas and sharing, and emotionally secure so that no one feels that they cannot openly share or ask questions (Yuan et al., 2018).

Now for the reality: The biggest barrier to planning collaboratively is finding time. Teachers and other school professionals are given planning time, but ensuring the planning time overlaps with those with whom you want to collaboratively plan is the trick. In order to determine with whom you should plan, ask yourself the following questions:

1. Are you a grade-level or content teacher? If yes, planning with other teachers in your grade level or content area can help you enhance your objectives, activities, and assessments. Additionally, by working together, it might save you some time in your own planning. If you are a teacher of subjects such as P.E., art, or music, it will be more challenging unless you have other teachers of your specialty in the building. Otherwise, collaborative planning will need to take the form of working with grade/content teachers, the entire team of various specialty teachers in the building, specialty teachers in your subject area in other schools, or with an instructional coach.

2. Do you have students with special needs in your class(es)? If yes, you should work with the special education teacher(s) overseeing the students' IEPs to meet their needs.

3. Do you have ELL students in your class(es)? If yes, planning with the ELL teacher can help you ensure your plans meet the needs of these students.

4. Do you have gifted students in your class(es)? If yes, planning with the gifted teacher can help you differentiate your plans to meet the needs of your high ability students.

It will be very challenging to meet with all these people in one meeting, so determine which group benefits the needs of your students—and you—the most. Begin there, then hold meetings with others as needed. For example, if you are a 4th grade teacher who teaches science, social studies, and math, your partnering teacher might be a colleague who teaches language arts. The biggest benefit would be to plan with the 4th grade team. Once you have your plans in place, meet with the special education teacher, ELL teacher, and gifted teacher to enhance your plans for these students. For another example, if you are a high school math teacher, the collaborative planning process may be as simple as working with the other mathematics teachers who can help you develop your plans most effectively.

🔧 Tools to Use

TOOL 19.1: Flowchart for Planning Collaboratively

This tool is a flowchart that can be used to show how to plan collaboratively.

How to Collaboratively Plan

Finding the best path for your team and your classroom

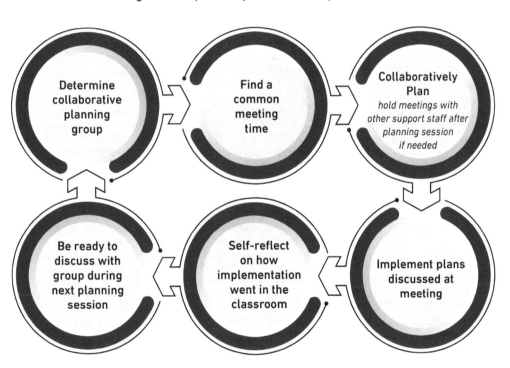

TOOL 19.2: Prioritize Planning Time

As stated above, the most challenging aspect of collaborative planning is time. This chart can help you prioritize your tasks as a teacher. It can be used daily or weekly to help you focus on what is most important. Remember: Planning collaboratively can benefit your professional development and help you complete your individual plans. Also, keep in mind that collaborative planning will save you time and effort in the long run. Hopefully, this chart helps you to recognize that, while there are many time-intensive tasks, the ebb and flow of priorities makes it manageable.

Considerations when looking at teacher time:
• Instruction
• Grading
• Staff meetings
• Parent meetings and calls
• Administrative duties (paperwork)
• Individual planning
• Professional development
• Collaborative planning
• Family responsibilities (before and after school)

Prioritize Your Time	
Top Priorities: 1. _____ 2. _____ 3. _____	Mid-Level Priorities: 1. _____ 2. _____ 3. _____
High-Level Priorities: 1. _____ 2. _____ 3. _____	Low-Level Priorities: 1. _____ 2. _____ 3. _____

Can you find common time with colleagues:
• Before school?
• After school?
• On a Zoom or Google Meet call?
• During lunch or recess?
• During special or enrichment periods?
• During your planning period?

TOOL 19.3: Preparing for Collaborative Planning

This template can be used to help you prepare for a collaborative planning session. It is important to come to the meetings prepared so that you get the most out of the collaborative time with your colleagues. Remember: Your colleagues' time is precious, and so is yours.

Self-Reflection	• How did your lesson plans and activities work out this week? • What worked well? • What did not work well?
Student Needs	• Were all student needs met? • How did support staff work with you to alter the collaborative plans to fit the needs of the individuals in your class?
Future Plans	• What ideas for activities do you have? • How will you break down the learning objectives? • What assessment will you use?
Ideas, Questions, or Concerns for the Group	

3

PART 4

Delivering Quality Instruction and Engaging Students in Learning

CHAPTERS 20-24

Focus on engaging your students cognitively through effective classroom techniques and using strategies to reach higher-level thinking skills.

20 Motivating Students to Learn

Motivating Students to Be Their Best

> **Words to Know**
>
> *Motivation*—the reason actions are taken or not taken as well as the forces or processes that instigate, guide, and sustain these actions

Motivating students to learn plays an extraordinarily powerful role in students' success. Motivation is one of the factors "stimulating, directing, and strengthening certain behavior, ensuring its repetition and continuity" (Engin, 2020, p. 258). Oftentimes the barriers between students and learning are psychological. When students are motivated, they are in a prime state to learn and integrate new information, and they are more receptive to and excited about learning. Conversely, when they are not motivated, they turn off. A 2017 poll of 5th through 12th graders found that only 47 percent of them feel engaged in schools, with 30 percent not engaged, and 23 percent actively disengaged (Gallup, 2018). And, unfortunately, when students move to higher grades, their excitement about what they are learning actually decreases.

For certain, student motivation is influenced by a number of family and personal variables, but schools and teachers play a vital and influential role as well. In fact, students' motivation to learn is highly susceptible to teacher intervention. For instance, the Gallup Student Poll (2018) found that students who strongly agreed with the statements "My school is committed to building the strengths of each student" and "I have at least one teacher who makes me excited about the future" were 30 times as likely as those who strongly disagreed with the statements to be motivated about learning (Gallup, 2018, p. 2). Thirty times!

On the other hand, research also suggests that boredom—the antithesis of motivation—has an overall effect size of −0.24 on student academic outcomes (i.e., a decrease of 9 percentile points) (Tze, Daniels, & Klassen, 2016). To avoid student boredom and the lack of engagement, we know that students are likely to be motivated to learn when they are given interesting and enjoyable tasks. Also, we know that holding high expectations and making available appropriate support are conducive to motivation. Research suggests that children are motivated to learn when they have confidence in their abilities and when they have a good relationship with the teacher. Effective teachers purposefully construct these conditions (Frenzel et al., 2019; Scales et al., 2020).

In an interesting experimental study, teachers gave written feedback on their 7th grade students' essays as they would normally do, such as giving suggestions for improvement or noting errors in spelling and grammar. However, later, the students were randomly assigned into two groups and the researchers appended a sticky note to each essay. For the treatment group, the note stated, "I'm giving you these comments because I have very high expectations and I know that you can reach them." And for the placebo group, the notes stated, "I'm giving you these comments so that you'll have feedback on your paper." The findings revealed that students in the first group were more likely to submit a revision of an essay and improve the quality of the final draft. And the positive impact of the motivating note was particularly strong with African American students. Seventy-two percent of African American students in the experimental group turned in a revision, compared to only 17 percent of those in the control group (Yeager et al., 2014). What a striking impact just by one encouraging note!

You probably already know about differences between intrinsic and extrinsic motivation. For a quick review, intrinsic motivation is related to the fact that humans typically want to understand the world, have control over their lives, and desire to be self-directed. Extrinsic motivation, such as external rewards, do have a role to play, especially in lower grades, but students may focus on the external rewards rather than seeing the inner value of the learning tasks. Thus, tapping into intrinsic motivation is more sustainable and rewarding, so it is important to help students explore their own personal reasons for working hard, and have answers for questions like "What's the value/use in the work?" and "Will I succeed and get the payoff [or results] if I take the needed actions?" To promote intrinsic motivation, students' perceived value and expectations of success are important. So, in classroom terms, teachers need to learn how to create academic environments in which students perceive themselves as being competent and autonomous (Brown, 2018).

🔧 Tools to Use

TOOL 20.1: Self-Assessment of Practices to Motivate Students

Use this self-assessment tool to give yourself feedback on your skills when it comes to motivating students. What are you doing well? What could you improve or add to motivate students in your classroom?

	I don't do this	Need to improve	Good	Excellent
I work to improve my students' positive beliefs about academic learning.				
I provide students with opportunities to experience success on different kinds of tasks so that they feel proud of themselves in mastering knowledge and skills.				
I use activities that are optimally challenging to allow students to move from what they already know and can do to the new learning objectives.				
I explicitly encourage students by letting them know that they have the needed competencies (e.g., prerequisite knowledge) to succeed in the new learning; if not, I provide reteaching.				
I point out to my students that their success in learning has to do with their effort and our actions do have a bearing on outcomes.				
I help students see the value of learning.				
I purposefully work to know my students and spend time talking with them about their interests, likes, areas of strength, and aspirations for the future.				
I help my students see the value in learning and connections between their learning and their world.				
I allow my students to have an appropriate amount of autonomy and choice about their learning while maintaining the rigor of their independent learning.				
I demonstrate that I truly care.				
I make sure that my students understand that I am here for them, and I provide support when they take learning risks.				
I shine a light on each student's strengths and create hope so they can believe in themselves and that they can achieve their dreams and goals in the future.				
I build relationships with my students that are based on trust and respect.				

4

TOOL 20.2: Scaffolding as a Form of Support and Motivation

In many situations, students are not motivated because they do not receive enough support, or scaffolding, to move on with learning. If we compare learning to mountain climbing, scaffolding would be the important "grips" that students can use to go up. What does scaffolding look like? Here are a few practices:

- Making connections among facts, ideas, and concepts

- Activating prior learning and facilitating students' recall and connection with previously learned materials

- Providing meaningful contexts for learning, such as anchoring the learning to real-life, authentic problems

- Asking probing questions to calibrate students' understanding and providing guidance tailored to helping them overcome misconceptions

- Increasing clarity in explanations—using examples to illustrate

- Providing just-in-time and personalized support to increase students' understanding

- Giving hints about effective strategies that students can use, or giving clues about new ways for thinking about a concept or approaching a problem

- Providing emotional support when needed, for instance, showing empathy or recognition that the new content is challenging, but it can be learned if given proper time and effort

- Rephrasing students' talk and engaging them in conversations to negotiate meanings and reach new understanding

- Modeling or demonstrating how to perform a difficult task

- Using graphic organizers in presenting complex information, such as using a Venn diagram to compare and contrast, sequencing graphics to sort out cause-effect relationships, providing a flow chart to illustrate process, or using a scoring rubric to clarify expectations

- Providing learning resources, such as templates, glossary with definitions of key vocabulary, examples, formula, and checklists

- Dividing a complex task into smaller manageable chunks

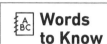
Words to Know

Scaffolding—the process of supporting students as they learn a new concept and as they become more independent removing that support

4

TOOL 20.3: Be Inspirational and Fun

Students who are inspired and having fun are motivated to learn! Use this list to reflect on why students might not be motivated and what steps you can take to change their attitudes. This list also provides some suggestions on how to inspire students and improve motivation with fun.

Encourage students to talk explicitly about why they should do their best in academic work and what is their hope for the future. Talk about why they should care.	Share anecdotes from your own personal history or others to motivate and inspire your students.	Take time to understand why some students are not motivated. Is it boredom? An urge to be rebellious? Or is the task beyond their abilities?
If the subject is boring to students, why is it so and how can it be changed? For example, ask yourself when, who, and how this theory or technique was developed? How has the world changed because of it? What real problems can it solve? Share your answers to those questions with your students using interesting stories and facts.	Bring inquiry and discovery into the learning.	Incorporate multimedia, music, and art into the learning.
Start the lesson with an interesting new story, game, court case, songs, provocative question, image, video, or demonstration.	Make sure every student has opportunities to contribute.	Be enthusiastic, as enthusiasm is contagious!

Keeping Your Students Engaged in Learning

21

CHAPTERCHAPTER

Student Engagement Promotes Student Learning

Anyone who has ever worked with students, no matter the age, know that engagement is vital to successful learning. While the term *engagement* may have you thinking about creative and fun activities in which your students participate, the engagement we are talking about is having students' minds intellectually engaged in learning. In fact, having fun in learning is an important part of engaging learners of any age. Engaged students are attentive, participative, and proactive. They are invested and enthusiastic about learning. They also persist longer and use more self-regulation to accomplish goals. They challenge themselves to exceed, and generally they gain more satisfaction from learning. On the other hand, disengaged students are more likely to avoid effort, withdraw from learning, have lower grades, and even drop out of school. Student engagement has a broad influence and is positively associated with desired academic, social, and emotional learning outcomes (Lei et al., 2018).

Research finds that teachers in highly engaged classrooms frequently display supportive practices (e.g., Dolezal et al., 2003; Konold et al., 2018), such as

- Dynamic presentations,

- Challenging and relevant activities,

- Communicating high expectations but also providing support, and

- Frequent feedback.

Conversely, there are certain classroom practices that compromise or even harm student engagement. Such undermining practices include poor classroom management characterized by frequent threats of punishment, lack of organization, poor planning, and simple, unchallenging tasks (Dennie et al., 2019).

🔧 Tools to Use

TOOL 21.1: Making the Learning Relevant to a Student's Real Life

When students experience learning as relevant to their present lives or future aspirations, that learning is more effective and more likely to stick, so it is important to help students understand why they are learning. When teachers use examples to tie the learning material to knowledge and skills, students can see the relevance of learning to their potential career future or what they are interested in, student engagement increases, and achievement outcomes improve (Schmidt et al., 2019). This tool can help you reflect on the lessons you teach for relevance.

☐ I clearly explain to students, "Why are we learning this?" "What does this have to do with me?"

☐ I anchor the new learning to everyday, real-life, and authentic problems.

☐ I elaborate on the significance and utility value of the new content.

☐ I try to find how the academic content relates to my students' experiences, cultures, interests, and future aspirations.

☐ I think from the perspective of my students and know their "scheme of things" to see how the new learning fits in their frame of reference.

TOOL 21.2: Giving the Right Amount of Challenge

Student engagement is associated with quality instruction that matches task complexities with individual skills. When an appropriate match occurs, students are more motivated and engaged, but when the task is not aligned to students' skill levels, engagement and motivation suffer (D'Mello, 2012). You may have heard the term *zone of proximal development* (Vygotsky, 1978)—the subtle area where the new learning is just beyond students' reach based on their current knowledge but can be accomplished with the teacher's assistance. When you can understand (either through observation or other assessments) what students already can do and what they cannot and then design the instruction in a way that effectively bridges the gap between these two, then your instruction is likely to be engaging and students will actually learn more effectively and accomplish their learning objectives. After teaching, reflect back on your lesson using these questions to ensure you are challenging students appropriately.

4

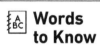

Words to Know

Zone of proximal development—the subtle area where the new learning is just beyond students' reach based on their current knowledge but can be accomplished with your assistance (Vygotsky, 1978)

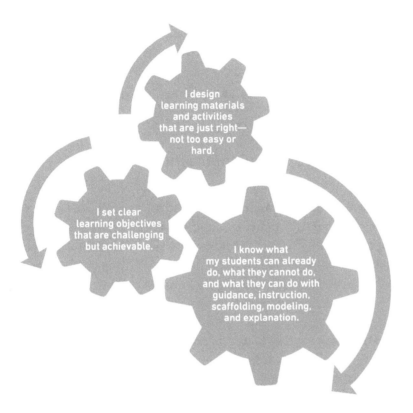

TOOL 21.3: Making Meaningful Connections

Effective teachers who are engaging often focus on forming meaningful connections between facts and ideas rather than delivering them as isolated pieces of information. Effective teachers present and engage students in content at various levels of complexity, using a broad range of objectives and activities that address both higher and lower levels of cognitive learning. Surface learning of factual knowledge is a necessary part of learning in any subject or content area, but the learning should not stop there. Students report greater interest, concentration, and enjoyment when completing tasks that require highly developed skills so that they have to actively think, understand, apply, evaluate, and create (Göçmençelebi et al., 2012; Ismail & Grossia, 2018). Additionally, effective teachers scaffold lessons to guide students in their emerging skills and knowledge acquisition through step-by-step instructions, modeling, and providing students with the opportunities to apply new information and skills to novel situations (Green et al., 2013). Ask yourself the following prompts as you reflect on your integration of meaningful connections:

☐ I ask probing questions and design activities that help students recall prior knowledge, form new connections, and make the new knowledge meaningful and memorable.

☐ I use graphic organizers and other strategies to illustrate the connections between concepts, facts, and ideas and demonstrate how they interconnect and build on one another as a coherent whole.

☐ I use larger, overarching, and valuable themes to give meaning to the curriculum content.

TOOL 21.4: Using a Variety of Instructional Strategies

Using a variety of instructional strategies, instead of depending on one or two, can make the learning more dynamic and interesting. The rich research on classroom teaching has helped shed light on what might be considered "high-yield strategies"—strategies that can potentially result in large increases in student achievement across a variety of subject areas and grade levels. However, it is important to remember that there is no magic formula or silver bullet that automatically yields engaging teaching. Picking the right strategies is contingent upon the subject content and your students' specific needs. Given the point that the learning context matters, it still would be helpful to keep the following lists of instructional strategies close as a quick reference. These strategies have been shown to be effective, in various instructional settings, by Marzano's and Hattie's meta-analyses of educational research (Hattie, 2009, 2017a; Marzano et al., 2001). The strategies with the largest effect are listed first.

Marzano's High-Yield Strategies	Hattie's High-Yield Strategies
Summarizing and note taking (1.00)	Integrating with prior knowledge (0.93)
Identifying similarities and differences (1.00)	Teaching students learning strategies (0.86)
Reinforcing effort and providing recognition (0.80)	Classroom discussion (0.82)
Homework and practice (0.77)	Scaffolding (0.82)
Nonlinguistic representations (0.75)	Concept mapping (0.64)
Cooperative learning (0.73)	Direct instruction (0.60)
Generating and testing hypotheses (0.61)	Mastery learning (0.57)
Setting objectives and providing feedback (0.61)	Incorporating technology (e.g., gaming, simulations, interactive video methods) (0.55)
Questions, cues, and advance organizers (0.59)	Inquiry-based learning and problem solving (0.40)

4

Note: Of course, there are many other instructional strategies that are valuable as learning tools and techniques for any good teacher to use, in fact Hattie lists more than 100!

Don't forget: Have a list of activities available in your personal repertoire that you want to use at the start and end of class as well as during classroom transitions. For instance, examples for starting the lesson might include beginning with a problem, a story, a mistake that captures student misconceptions, a video, or a movement; closing activities might include the lesson using an exit ticket or asking students to generate an elevator pitch under 60 seconds to summarize what they have learned.

TOOL 21.5: Tapping into Various Cognitive Levels

In order to engage students, you not only need solid knowledge about the subject matter and pedagogy, but you also need to know your students in terms of their readiness for the learning and the individual differences they bring to the classroom. One way to help you organize, represent, and adapt learning activities to suit your students' needs, abilities, and preferences include varying the cognitive complexity of the learning based on Bloom's revised taxonomy (Anderson & Krathwohl, 2001) and Webb's depth of knowledge (Webb, 1997). This approach to customizing classroom experiences rather than using uniform strategies across all lessons and for all students is much more aligned with building better student engagement.

Bloom's revised taxonomy and Webb's depth of knowledge will help you think of learning from different levels of complexity and depth. Only the instruction that is designed with student learning needs and strengths in consideration will allow students to work at their optimal level and promote growth. If your teaching can serve the broad spectrum of learning needs and strengths, the content will be better delivered—and better learned!

4

Bloom's Revised Taxonomy

Remembering	Recalling previously learned information
Understanding	Demonstrating an understanding of facts; explaining ideas or concepts
Applying	Using information in another familiar fashion; executing and implementing skills
Analyzing	Differentiating and organizing information into parts to explore the relations of ideas, such as the relative hierarchy
Evaluating	Justifying a decision or course of action; judging based on given criteria; making decisions
Creating	Generating new or original ideas, products, or ways of viewing things

Source: Information from Anderson & Krathwohl (2001).

Webb's Depth of Knowledge

Level	Label	Actions
1	Recall and Reproduction	Recall, recite, repeat, draw, list, label, recognize, etc.
2	Skills and Concepts	Graph, classify, separate, organize, infer, describe, predict, etc.
3	Strategic Thinking and Reasoning	Revise, assess, explain, formulate, draw conclusions, critique, etc.
4	Extended Thinking	Design, synthesize, create, prove, connect, etc.

Source: Information from Webb (1997).

4

Making Homework Actually Work

To Give or Not to Give Homework

As a new—or relatively new—teacher, it may seem overwhelming to think about creating assignments for students to complete beyond your classroom—in other words, homework. Homework can be complicated when you factor in the role parents may play (or not play) and consider what role homework will have in your assessment of students' understanding of content and skills. Yet, homework does play an important role in instruction and assessment, and determining how to use it effectively to the benefit of students and student achievement is important. Thus, homework, if used to its maximum benefit, is something that will require your thoughtful and continuing attention.

Homework has been a mainstay in American education for about as far back as we can document. However, since a 1989 study by Cooper, the use of homework has come under scrutiny, particularly with students at the elementary level. While it is true that homework has a smaller effect size (0.29) than many other instructional strategies, the effect size is greater for older students and, when used as an extension of the classroom, it embodies an important and effective part of teaching and learning (Hattie, 2017; Stronge, 2018). More recent studies find that students' perceptions on the quality of homework plays a role in its effectiveness on student achievement, including in elementary schools (Fan et al., 2017; Rosário et al., 2018). What does seem clear is that quality homework, accompanied by quality feedback on the homework, plays an important role in student achievement.

> **Words to Know**
>
> *Homework*—schoolwork assigned while in school that is to be completed outside of school hours

Assigning Homework

You have a vital role in the process of homework, from its design to managing and monitoring its implementation and reviewing it (Fitzmaurice et al., 2020). Because it takes time and effort to assign homework, you want to ensure that what you assign is supporting and not discouraging student learning (Dean et al., 2012). Teachers usually assign homework for one of three purposes: 1) as a way to monitor students' progress on skills or content taught in class, 2) as an extension of the skills or content taught

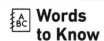

Words to Know

Extension—an assignment or activity that requires students to use knowledge or skills learned in a new way or to apply it to real world situations

in class, or 3) as a way to help students prepare for future instruction in the classroom (Rosário et al., 2015). Additionally, homework that has the purpose of extending learning and focuses on problem solving has a positive effect on student achievement (Rosario et al., 2015; Stronge, 2018; Zhu & Leung, 2012). While this is true, most teachers assign homework to help students practice or drill (Bang, 2012; Danielson et al., 2011), which has been found to have a negative impact on school achievement (Rosário et al., 2015; Trautwein et al., 2009). Therefore, ensuring that you are thoughtful in your assignment of homework has a vital effect on its value. While certain student characteristics, such as time management, self-regulation, and motivation, may influence whether students complete homework or not, extension homework is seen by students as academically demanding and has been found to motivate students to complete it when it is carefully and thoughtfully planned (Dettmers et al., 2010).

⚒ Tools to Use

TOOL 22.1: The Teacher's Role When Assigning Homework

While it would be nice to think that assigning homework is as simple as giving students the suggested homework from the textbook, planning for worthwhile homework is more nuanced and should be structured to support and extend classroom learning. To ensure this happens, the teacher must design quality homework, help students, describe how to implement homework, and acknowledge the time and effort of students by assessing the homework. These phases of the homework process ensure that neither you nor the students are wasting time completing work that does not make a difference in their learning.

Design	• Determine the purpose for assigning homework.
	• Take into account your time, the curriculum, and school or district regulations.
	• Choose appropriate subject matter, ensuring the difficulty level matches the purpose in assigning the homework.
	• Differentiate homework for students based on their differing abilities and learning needs.
	• Make the homework interesting, stimulating, engaging, enjoyable, experiential, and/or creative.
	• Make sure the homework has a connection to what is happening in the classroom.
	• Check with other teachers in the grade level to ensure students are not receiving too much homework at the same time.
Implement	• Clearly explain to students the purpose behind the homework to be completed.
	• Give instructions to both parents and students on how much help families should provide to students when completing the homework.
	• Communicate expectations for completing homework and the consequences for not doing so.
	• Assign the homework in a manner that creates a regular, but still fresh, pattern.
Assess	• Assess the homework using a combination of methods such as individualized, self, peer, or group correction.
	• Make sure students receive feedback that is meaningful.
	• Homework should be used as a type of formative assessment but not count toward end-of-course grades.
	• Remember: If there is no assessment and timely feedback, the value of homework diminishes dramatically.

Source: Information from Bembenutty (2011); Fitzmaurice et al. (2020); Holte (2016); Vatterott (2018).

4

TOOL 22.2: Teacher Homework Self-Assessment and Reflection Worksheet

Because the homework process can be complex and can make an impact on students' academic achievement, it is important to make sure you are addressing proper design, implementation, and assessment methods. If a parent or student were to ask, "Why did I do that homework?" you will have a thoughtful answer.

Question	Reflections
What is the purpose of the assignment?	
Do I know what other home-work students have for other classes/subjects?	
What will the students gain from completing this homework?	
Can the students complete this homework independently?	
If parents are going to help, what kind of help is appropriate?	
Can the students be success-ful in the class without this homework? If yes, how do you know?	
How much homework am I giving? Is it enough to meet the purpose and not too much to overwhelm?	
Are there other school events going on that might limit students' ability to complete homework on the day/night assigned?	
What are the consequences for not completing the homework?	

4

TOOL 22.3: Homework Survey

Use this tool to glean more information about your students' access to and availability of resources as you consider the type and volume of homework you assign.

Student Name:
Please describe your internet access at home:
When you complete homework or projects, who is available at home to assist you?
When/where do you typically complete your homework?
List anything that may make it difficult to complete your homework:

4

23 Engaging Students with Classroom Discussions

Creating Rich Classroom Discussions

Classroom discussions is a powerful instructional strategy that shifts the responsibility of learning and thinking to students. Using classroom discussion empowers and supports "students' ability to think and decide for themselves, which is critical in the 21st century where the widespread proliferation of information and knowledge means that there is an ever increasing need for learners to sift through layers of (mis/dis) information" (Teo, 2019, p. 10). Classroom discussions also play an influential role in helping students explore and examine issues, and they help to shape students' egalitarian attitudes (Carrasco & Irribarra, 2018). Teachers should consider how to optimally integrate discussions into instruction because of the opportunities it provides for learners.

Research affirms that classroom discussions are positively associated with supporting learning goals across content areas (e.g., Banes et al., 2018; Gillies, 2016). Classroom discussions are associated with an effect size of 0.82, which is equivalent to a 29 percentile point gain in student achievement (Hattie, 2017a). Classroom discussions benefit linguistically diverse students as well as their native speaking peers (Banes et al., 2018).

Supporting classroom discussion involves cultivating the classroom conditions and purposefully preparing for the discussion. "With thoughtful and well-designed discussion tasks, teachers can help students attain learning goals of critical inquiry, debate and reflection" (Ngeow & Kong, 2003, p. 4). For this discussion-oriented approach to take hold, students need to feel safe in the classroom environment so they can express their thoughts and opinions, invent, create, take risks, and dig for deeper meaning (McKee, 2015). Teachers and students, alike, should respect, value, and be attentive to what students say. It is also important to maintain an environment that promotes student responsibility and orchestrates discourse that includes multiple students discussing topics together.

Tools to Use

Classroom discussion can be an effective strategy to deepen student understanding by encouraging students to suspend judgment, offer new ideas, weigh alternatives, and consider different points of view. Initially, it can be intimidating, but once your students and you feel comfortable and are used to this strategy, it can be an enlightening and effective instructional tool (Wassermann, 2010). We have included a few tools here that may help you bring classroom discussions to life in your classroom.

TOOL 23.1: Exit Ticket for Class Discussions

Use this tool as an exit ticket for having students reflect on class discussions. It also helps inform you about students' perspectives and provides an opportunity for you to be aware of unanswered questions students may have as a result of a discussion.

Student name:	
Provide a quick summary of the topic discussed today.	
What is one thing you (circle one) **agreed with** or **disagreed with** and why?	
What is one follow-up question you have from today's discussion?	

4

TOOL 23.2: Types of Classroom Discussion

Like many other instructional techniques, student discussion comes in many forms. This tool lists a number of commonly used discussion formats. You can determine which approach to use according to the learning objectives and the amount of time you have. For instance, problem-solving discussion might be extensive and include the full range of components, such as identifying a problem, analyzing a problem, evaluating potential solutions, and decision making. However, a problem-solving discussion also can be abbreviated to just involve formulating hypotheses or predicting probable consequences. So ultimately you have options, and you can decide what works best in the particular teaching context.

Policy Discussion	Discussion that focuses on students' reactions toward certain issues and requires them to take a stand and defend that position.
Problem-Solving Discussion	Discussion that requires groups of students to seek an answer or solution to a problem.
Cause-Effect Discussion	Discussion that prompts students to analyze and articulate a cause-effect relationship.
Predicting Discussion	Discussion that leads students to predict the probable consequences of a given situation, position, or action.
Questioning the Author	Discussion that is usually used to develop students' understanding of a text. In this process, teachers form questions while reading a given text to spark student thinking and discussion. Examples might include "What is the author trying to say?" "Why does the author choose the characters and the settings?" or "How does the author feel about the topic?"
Think-Pair-Share	A more informal way of discussion where students work in pairs to think aloud and solve a problem or answer a question and then share ideas with classmates.
Gallery Walk	Flip-chart papers with questions are posted around the room, and students in small groups rotate among the posters to discuss and write their answer on the papers. Synthesizing or summary discussion can ensue once the students complete the posting process.
Socratic Seminar	Socratic seminar is a more formal way of student discussion where students must be prepared with prereading and annotating text and discussion questions. Usually, the students sit in a circle so that they make eye contact, and they need to support opinions with textual evidence. They direct comments to one another (not the teacher).

4

TOOL 23.3: Reflecting on and Assessing Classroom Discussions

Use this tool as you reflect on the discussion you had in your classroom with your students. This reflection will help you in the future to improve the quality of these discussions and further improve student learning.

1. First of all, how can you better incorporate student discussion into your particular subject area and grade? Effective classroom discussion is often purposeful, and discussion should be designed to contribute deliberately to instruction and learning. For discussion to work well as an instructional strategy, it should be aligned with the learning objectives of your lesson.

2. How would you assess or evaluate your use of student discussion in your classroom? Specifically, evaluate yourself along the recommended practices:

   • Start the discussion by posing an open-ended, thematic, and intriguing question that has no obvious right or wrong answer but genuinely puzzles students and will solicit different points of view.

   • Clarify the rules and expectations for discussion from the outset.

   • Encourage attentive, respectful listening.

   • Allow students to explore diverse perspectives.

3. Specifically, how do you evaluate your practices of preparing and starting a discussion, facilitating a discussion, and concluding one? How might you improve your use of discussion in your teaching?

4

TOOL 23.4: Student Self-Assessment of Classroom Discussions

Student self-assessment can play a role in helping students become reflective about their participation in the discussion. Consider using the criteria in this tool to create a student self-assessment rubric and share it with students before the discussion.

	Never	Rarely	Sometimes	Often	Always
Preparation					
Do I come to class prepared to participate in class discussions?					
Do I have questions based on the homework or classwork given?					
Do I have evidence of my claims for discussion based on the homework or readings?					
Participation					
Do I raise my hand in class to participate?					
Do my class contributions add to the discussions?					
Do I monopolize the classroom discussion?					
Reasoning					
Do I cite evidence for my claims?					
Do I help move conversations forward by presenting new thoughts/ideas?					
Do I clearly articulate my ideas so that my classmates understand?					
Do I disagree respectfully with those who think differently than I do?					

4

	Never	Rarely	Sometimes	Often	Always
Listening					
Do I pay attention to what my classmates say?					
Do I base my comments off what others have said?					
Do I show listening behaviors while others are speaking?					

TOOL 23.5: How to Start and Facilitate Classroom Discussions

Knowing how to begin a focused classroom discussion feels like it should be second nature to a teacher, but it takes more than just talking to the students. Use these strategies to help you as you begin thinking about the ideal classroom discussion you envision for your students.

4

Strategies to start a classroom discussion:

- Begin by considering what objectives you want to accomplish through a student discussion and using a question that has no easy yes/no answer but has clear bearing on the subject matter.

- Come to a consensus on the rules for participation, listening, and acceptable ways to interact. It is important to clarify that students are supposed to direct questions to each other rather than always going through you.

- Establish or have students brainstorm accepted criteria of good reasoning and communication. Clarify how the assessment of the discussion will work if it will be conducted.

- Use a common experience, a newspaper story, a film, a quote, a demonstration, or a role play to help students link the discussion to their own lives and what they are learning.

- Ask students ahead of time to write one or two open-ended questions about their reading, and then you can categorize the questions thematically and assign them to students in small groups or for discussion as an entire class.

- Be benignly controversial by selecting a debatable issue where students have to pick a side about the issue so they can have at least "forced disagreement," and then they need to argue objectively both sides of the topic.

Strategies to facilitate classroom discussion:

- Model or prompt students to build on others' comments, for instance, by pointing out what is interesting or compelling in the comments and explaining why they agree or disagree with the comments. Being specific is the key here.

- Model or prompt students to be good listeners, for instance, by making eye contact, asking follow-up questions to seek clarification or elaboration on a point that is not clear, or paraphrasing a point that is heard and then building on it.

- Model or prompt students to disagree respectfully and constructively, for instance, by synthesizing others' comments first to show they have listened carefully and then presenting a different view.

- Model or prompt students to write down notes of others' comments or even create a graphic organizer to keep track of the main points and thread of discussion.

- Model or prompt students to summarize and express appreciation for the insights they have gained from the discussion.

- Silence is OK. When silence occurs, give students a few moments to formulate their thoughts or write down responses. Also, when silence occurs, you can summarize student responses without taking a side.

- When a few students start to dominate the discussion, slow down the pace and invite the quieter students to speak up.

Providing Effective Student Feedback

Quality Feedback Impacts Student Learning

Providing timely, specific, and actionable feedback is one of the crucial instructional tools that helps students learn—and learn best (Erturan-Ilker, 2014). Students' learning is influenced by feedback in multiple ways, including increased effort, motivation, engagement, and positive perceptions of the learning climate (Erturan-Ilker, 2014; Senko & Harackiewicz, 2005). Feedback can help confirm what is correct or incorrect in student learning by exposing and addressing student misconceptions in a content area or a skill set. It also helps students learn about alternative strategies, take new directions, and identify extra information to advance their learning (Hattie, 2009; Stronge & Xu, 2016).

Providing feedback to students has a powerful impact on student learning. Hattie's (2017a) synthesis of research on feedback finds an overall effect size of 0.70, which is equivalent to an achievement gain of 26 percentile points. However, research also suggests that the effect of feedback varies considerably depending on how the feedback is given and received (Hattie & Timperley, 2007; Ocak & Karafil, 2020). Research actually suggests that simply telling students whether their answers are right or wrong has a negative impact on learning (Marzano et al., 2001). Typically, feedback that provides specific information on students' performance on task, product, process, and self-regulation is more effective than feedback that comments solely on correctness of student work (Guo & Wei, 2019; Hattie, 2009). Also, the feedback that provides learning-goal-related cues and reinforcement is more powerful than the feedback that does not provide concrete information (Hattie, 2009).

When we provide the correct or wrong answer without offering prompts to extend students' thinking, the feedback has only a small positive effect.

However, if the teacher explains what is accurate and what is inaccurate in student responses, then the feedback has a bigger impact. Furthermore, feedback that encourages students to keep trying until they succeed is effective as well (Marzano et al., 2001).

When giving feedback, effective teachers avoid simple yes or no answers; rather, they provide content-specific explanations of what students are doing correctly, what

 Words to Know

Feedback—the process of giving information about a student's performance on a task or activity which is used to improve performance

they are not doing correctly, and how to address the errors (Baliram & Ellis, 2019; Hargreaves, 2019). Hattie and Timperley (2007, p. 87) structured three questions to guide feedback:

1. Where am I going?
2. How am I going?
3. Where to next?

Feedback on the first question helps clarify learning goals and intentions. Feedback answering the second question provides information on students' current task performance. Feedback targeting the last question provides informative guidance or cues for improvement and progress toward the desired performance. Students are more likely to use feedback to improve their learning when the feedback is constructive and when it clarifies their doubts, indicates the quality of their work, prompts them to elaborate their ideas, or provides specific examples that help them think more deeply (Guo & Wei, 2019; Hattie, 2012). Effective feedback pinpoints the gap between students' current task performance and the desired learning outcomes.

⚒ Tools to Use

TOOL 24.1: Essential Characteristics of Feedback

Feedback can serve various purposes. There are several widely known elements that make feedback effective when used by teachers (Wiggins, 2012). This tool is built on these elements. Additionally, there are several widely known elements that make feedback effective when used by teachers (Wiggins, 2012). This tool will help you determine if your feedback is focused and contains those effective elements.

Desired Elements	Try to Avoid	Very dissatisfied	Not satisfied	Satisfied	Very satisfied
Goal-referenced: Make reference to learning goals, objectives, and criteria of quality performance.	Feedback that is marginal to what students are learning; imprecise feedback that makes students have to guess what is expected of them				
Specific: Evidence-based and informative explanations of what students are doing well and not doing well	Correct-or-wrong and yes-or-no feedback; comments that are vague				
Timely: Give feedback when it is most needed; also start giving feedback before assignments are due so that students have opportunities to improve and you do not need to give feedback on everything for everybody at the same time when the assignments are due.	Delayed feedback that is no longer related to what students are presently learning				
Actionable: Feedback that leads students to try alternative strategies or to seek out additional resources to develop their understanding and skills Note: One strategy to make sure the feedback is read and used by students is to give written feedback while holding onto the grades, and allow students to digest the feedback and resubmit their revised work before giving the final scores.	Feedback that does not give guidance on what to do next, or that is too prescriptive, leaving no room for students' own decision making				
User-friendly: Feedback is communicated in a way that can be easily understood by the students and feedback that is customized to each student's learning.	Feedback that lacks clarity and is hard to understand				
Constructive and positive: Offer feedback in a constructive manner, which means being positive about the strengths in students, using an encouraging tone, but also being impactful enough to drive students to improve. This also means that mistakes are wonderful opportunities to learn, rather than reasons to feel stupid, inadequate, embarrassed, and disappointed about oneself.	Comments that are overly negative, putting students down, and making students believe they do not have potential to achieve; comments that make students feel fearful of taking risks and avoid tasks, rather than having a desire to reflect on and fix the mistakes				

4

TOOL 24.2: Sentence Stems You Can Use for Feedback

Sometimes knowing what to say to students is the most important skill in providing effective feedback and guiding their next steps. These sentence stems can help you build responses to students in different situations.

- "You got this problem wrong. That actually is fantastic! Mistakes give valuable opportunities to learn. And let's see what we can learn from this one."

- "Your introduction paragraph is particularly strong because . . . ."

- "I have difficulty following the logic in the third paragraph because . . . ."

- "Do you remember what we are trying to master for today's learning?"

- "Is there anything else you can try?"

- "What will you do next?"

- "How will you proceed?"

- "Perhaps you can extend this section by further addressing . . . ."

- "Have you considered . . . ?"

- "When you said . . . , am I correct understanding that you meant to say . . . ?"

- "Let's compare the steps you used with the example. What differences do you see?"

- "You might want to support your argument by using information from this resource . . . ."

4

TOOL 24.3 Observation and Reflection on Feedback

Use this observation form to record the verbal feedback you provide in class. You may ask a colleague to observe you and write down the statements you used, or you can record your own teaching and use the form to reflect.

Topic Areas (Check one)	Essential Characteristics (Check all that apply)	Your Feedback Statement	How did students respond to your feedback?	How can you improve your feedback?
☐ Goals of learning ☐ High-quality performance ☐ Changes students can make to improve learning	☐ Goal-referenced ☐ Specific ☐ Timely ☐ Actionable ☐ User-friendly ☐ Constructive and positive			
☐ Goals of learning ☐ High-quality performance ☐ Changes students can make to improve learning	☐ Goal-referenced ☐ Specific ☐ Timely ☐ Actionable ☐ User-friendly ☐ Constructive and positive			
☐ Goals of learning ☐ High-quality performance ☐ Changes students can make to improve learning	☐ Goal-referenced ☐ Specific ☐ Timely ☐ Actionable ☐ User-friendly ☐ Constructive and positive			

4

PART 5

Assessment of and for Learning

CHAPTERS 25–28

Ensure that your planning and instruction are meeting the goals and objectives you set for your students.

Collecting Student Learning Data Through Quality Classroom Assessments

Quality Assessments Give an Accurate Picture of Student Learning

Classroom assessments are important because they provide essential information about students' progress, which can help you make decisions about your instruction more quickly and more accurately. Because assessment data are vital to decision making, it makes sense that the data collected should be as useful as possible. Using formative and summative assessment, you will have a variety of data available. Formative assessment gives you information as to where students are in their learning process and what changes need to be made to their instruction as a result. Therefore, ensuring the data give a true picture of student learning is vital. Likewise, summative assessment gives a full picture of student learning on a topic to ensure students have met the learning objective(s). The data from this type of assessment need to be of good quality so that when it comes to next steps, you are well informed.

As a teacher you have many resources at hand to serve as assessments of student learning—including textbook-provided materials and tests passed around by grade levels or subject areas—but these tools will not always give you a full picture of student learning. While there are many assessment tools readily available to you, it is better to focus on assessing what is important for the students to know, as this knowledge will give you a more accurate picture of what your students have learned and still need to learn (Stronge et al., 2017). Once you have accurate data on student knowledge, then you can use this information as feedback to help you design instruction to meet students' needs.

Experienced teachers often prefer to write their own assessments to evaluate students (DiDonato-Barnes et al., 2014); however, if students are assessed with poorly designed assessments, knowing what a student has learned is not possible. It has been shown that only about 60 percent of assessment items are technically acceptable or better (Quaigrain & Arhin, 2017). So, valid assessment data = accurate knowledge of student progress.

Processes to Creating Quality Classroom Assessments

When developing classroom assessments, it is important to think about the functionality and utility of the assessment. Thinking through these types of questions can help you thoughtfully design meaningful classroom assessments.

- What content am I planning to assess?
- What skills do I plan to assess?
- How much time is available for the assessment?
- Will I use the information formatively or summatively?
- Will I assign grades for the assessment?
- If students are working together, how will I know what students contributed individually?
- Is there an existing assessment that has been created that I can use as a reference?
- What does mastery look like for this assessment?
- What will I do with the assessment results?

🔧 Tools to Use

TOOL 25.1: Assessment Item Categories

This tool breaks down the most common types of assessment items into categories based on how students typically respond and then considers the cognitive level used most typically for each assessment type. Of course, there are exceptions to the typical uses.

5

Assessment Items						
Select Response			Supply Response			Performance Response
Matching	Multiple Choice	True/ False	Fill-in- the- Blank	Short Answer	Essay	Performance Task

Bloom's Cognitive Levels		Matching	Multiple Choice	True/ False	Fill-in-the-Blank	Short Answer	Essay	Performance Task
	Remember	x	x	x	x			
	Understand	x	x	x	x			
	Apply		x			x	x	x
	Analyze					x	x	x
	Evaluate					x	x	x
	Create						x	x

Source: Adapted from Stronge & Associates (2018).

TOOL 25.2: Pros and Cons of Assessment Types

This chart shows the pros and cons of using each category. Tool 25.1 can help you determine what assessment type is best for your needs. When creating an assessment, of course, you will need to use your judgment based on the cognitive level of the learning objectives, the amount of time you have to spend on the assessment, and on grading.

5

	Pros	Cons
Select Response	• If designed properly, grading is not subjective, as the answer is either correct or incorrect. • Easy and quick to grade. • Best when used for objectives with lower cognitive levels.	• Students can guess to get a correct answer, which does not help the teacher know if the student has learned the concept. • It is difficult to write questions at higher cognitive levels.
Supply Response	• Gives students a chance to show what they know in depth. • Allows students to react to the material presented. • Good choice for assessing higher cognitive levels.	• The open-ended nature of these questions can lead to subjectivity. Using a rubric when grading is recommended. • Can be time-intensive to grade and give quality feedback.
Performance Task	• Allows for student participation in real-life situations. • Allows student choice and the chance to individualize their learning. • Good choice for assessing higher cognitive levels.	• Subjective in nature and should be graded with a rubric. • Can take a long time for students to complete the task.

Source: Information from Clay (2001); Gareis & Grant (2015); Stronge & Associates (2018); Zimmaro (2016).

 **Words to Know**

Performance task—a task where students must demonstrate their knowledge and learning by performing a specified task

Select response—students must choose the correct response from the choices given

Supply response—students create and provide their own answers

TOOL 25.3: Assessment Question Items and Tips

This chart analyzes each assessment item and offers tips on how to write a question of that type as well as some helpful examples.

5

Select Response	
Matching	• Should be a short matching set. • Order choices logically (e.g., ABC, chronological). • Use short stems. • Provide more answers than stems so process of elimination does not impact the data. • Use content that is homogeneous (e.g., dates with dates and people with people, don't mix). • There should be only one answer for each stem. **Good Example:** Determine where Native Americans have lived by matching the tribe to where they lived. ____ Lived in the Artic 1.) Lakota ____ Lived in the Northwest 2.) Pueblo ____ Lived on the Plains 3.) Cherokee ____ Lived in the Southwest 4.) Iroquois ____ Lived in the Eastern Woodlands 5.) Inuit 6.) Kwakiutl The example uses short stems which are all homogeneous and provides an extra answer response to prevent students from using the process of elimination.
Multiple Choice	**The Stem:** The stem is the question portion. • The stem should clearly and directly state the problem. • Use only a single idea in each item. • When using qualifiers like *most likely*, make them stand out. • Avoid the use of negatives or double negatives. State the item in the positive whenever possible. **The Answer:** The answer refers to the answer choices. • Be sure wrong answer choices are plausible. • Include 3–5 answer options. • The length of each answer choice should be about the same (preferably short). • Avoid using "All of the Above" and "None of the Above." • Ensure the correct answer is the only viable correct answer. • Place answers in an order that makes sense (e.g., numerical, ABC). • Avoid giving clues in the answer choices. **Good Example:** Read the sentence from *The Heart of Darkness*: "Hunters for gold or pursuers of fame, they all had gone out on that stream, bearing the sword, and often the torch, messengers of the might within the land, bearers of a spark from the sacred fire." (Conrad, 1990, p. 2) When the narrator makes this observation, what do the sword and torch have to do with a story about Africa? A) Freedom B) Imperialism C) War The example is a short stem and answer. Answer choices are in alphabetical order and there are 3–5 plausible choices.

	Select Response—(*continued*)
True/False	• Use one central idea in each true/false statement. • Make sure the statement is unquestionably true or false. • Avoid using the words always and never. • Avoid using the terms seldom, often, and many. • Avoid using negatives or double negatives. State the item in the positive whenever possible. **Good Example:** The Bill of Rights is the first 10 amendments to the Constitution. The example has a central idea and does not include any modifiers or qualifiers.
	Supply Response
Fill-in-the-Blank	• Place the blank near or at the end of the statement. • Keep blanks an equal length. • Use your own words and do not copy statements directly from sources the students studied. • Do not give grammatical cues (use a[n] instead of a or an). • Omit only significant words from the statement and not so many words that the intended meaning is lost. • Make sure there is only one correct response. **Good Example:** In the year 1819, Thomas Jefferson created a charter for _____. This example is short, includes only one correct response, has the blank at the end, and does not give any grammatical clues.
Short Answer and Essay	• Create questions based on important concepts, objectives, and standards. • Make sure students have enough space to respond. • Create a rubric to score each item. • Detail how students should respond (e.g., paragraphs, bullet points, phrases, complete sentences). • Make sure to indicate partial scores for partial answers. • Avoid using long complex explanations to ask the questions. **Good Example:** Short Answer: Analyze the reasons the United States entered World War I. Essay: Write a five-paragraph essay comparing and contrasting the leadership of Franklin Roosevelt and Winston Churchill during World War II. Both examples are concrete in what they expect from the students. The statements are short and concise. The teacher created a rubric prior to administering this assessment.

5

Supply Response—*(continued)*	
Performance Task	• The task should be open-ended. • Remind students that there are multiple correct answers. • Give students the evaluation criteria prior to beginning the project. • Make sure the task provides evidence of learning the material at the desired cognitive level (e.g., understand, apply, analyze). • Give students the opportunity to apply their knowledge in a variety of ways. • Create authentic and novel contexts for the task. • Try to incorporate multiple subjects or multiple 21st century skills in the task. **Good Example:** The release of the movie *Blackfish* in 2013 raised the awareness of many to orca whales in captivity specifically in educationally based aquariums. Research the issue and make a presentation on your point of view of keeping orca whales captive for the purpose of education and teaching of environmental issues. You may present your perspective in any way you choose, just remember to use the rubric as you work. Additionally, you may choose to work individually or in a small group. This example allows students to choose how they present their perspective based on the research they have completed. It incorporates 21st century skills as well as higher level cognitive learning. Lastly, the problem is current and has students investigating a real-world ethical dilemma.

Source: Information from Brame (2013); Clay (2001); Gareis & Grant (2015); Hartell & Strimel (2018); Stronge & Associates (2018); Zimmaro (2016).

TOOL 25.4: Analyzing Teacher-Made Assessments

Teachers often write their own assessments, which is more challenging than you might expect. This tool is a quiz for students in grades 2–4. It covers objectives at the remember and understand level as the teacher assesses vocabulary and whether students can recognize everyday items as simple machines. It has been analyzed using the information from the chart in Tool 25.2 to determine if the questions are well-written.

Because this assessment is written like a fill-in-the-blank but is really a matching assessment, a more effective way to create the same assessment would be like the example below. Writing the assessment like this example would give you a better understanding of whether students learned the material. The matching includes homogenous content, alphabetized lists, and an extra term to prevent students from using the process of elimination.

Name _____

Word Bank

Force	Screw	Compound Machine
Work	Inclined Plane	Wheel and Axle
Machine	Wedge	Simple Machine
Pulley	Lever	Energy

> While this assessment looks like a fill-in-the-blank or a supply response, it is really a matching assessment due to having a word bank.

1 _____ is the ability to do work.

2. A _____ is a simple machine that uses a wheel and a rope. A flagpole is an example.

3. _____ is the force that changes the motion of an object.

4. An _____ is a flat surface that is raised at one end. A ramp is an example.

> There are more answers than choices which is good, but the words in the bank are not in a logical order.

5. A _____ is a machine with few or no moving parts.

6. A _____ is an inclined plane wrapped into a spiral. A propeller is an example.

7. A _____ is a straight bar that moves on a fixed point. A seesaw is an example.

8. A _____ is two or more simple machines put together.

9. A _____ is a tool that makes work easier to do.

> All the matching content is homogenous.

10. A _____ is a wheel that turns on a post. A wagon is an example.

Name _____

Match the word on the right with its definition.

____ the ability to do work

____ the force that changes the motion of an object

____ two or more simple machines put together

____ the speed of something in a given direction

____ a tool that makes work easier to do

____ a machine with few or no moving parts

1. Compound Machine
2. Energy
3. Machine
4. Simple Machine
5. Velocity
6. Work

Match the word on the left with the item on the right that is its example.

1. Gear

2. Incline Plane

3. Lever

4. Pulley

5. Screw

6. Wedge

7. Wheel and Axel

____ a flagpole

____ a ramp

____ a jar lid

____ a seesaw

____ an axe

____ a water well

26 Preparing Students for Standardized Tests

Two Birds, One Stone

The accountability era of education in the United States was a key focus of the *No Child Left Behind Act* (NCLB) in 2002 and continues to exist today with the *Every Student Succeeds Act* (ESSA) (Jeasik et al., 2020). This leads to students spending approximately 33 days—or one day out of every six—testing and often devoting more time to prepare for these tests (Jeasik et al., 2020). A focus on testing leaves a lot less time for teachers to meet their curriculum goals and objectives and prepare students for these high-stakes tests. While teachers see the need for assessment, including standardized tests, the washback effect has a profound impact on classrooms (Gebril & Eid, 2017; Kinay & Ardic, 2017). As a consequence, there is a bit of a conundrum: Teachers sometimes feel the tension between motivating students for learning and, at the same time, preparing them for standardized tests (Shelton & Brooks, 2019). As a teacher, it will be necessary to be able to take care of these two birds—that is, engaging and motivating teaching and test preparation—with one stone! But how?

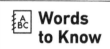

Words to Know

Washback effect— the effect of tests on teaching and learning

Preparing Students for Standardized Tests

While the thought of taking standardized tests can be anxiety-producing for students and teachers alike, it is not likely to end in the near future—not in school and probably not in life after school. So as a teacher you need to find a way to prepare your students for these tests but also use the best practices you were taught in school. In terms of preparing students, it might feel unnatural, scripted, and teaching to the test; however, you are preparing students for a future where medical schools, law schools, and even many vocational schools require tests that students must pass prior to practicing their given craft in service of the community. Below is a good look at the benefits of performing test preparation in the classroom, the drawbacks, and different types of test preparation you might choose to use (Gebril & Eid, 2017).

Benefits:

- Providing psychological support to students by familiarizing them with the test format, which can help alleviate anxiety and increase confidence.

- Improving test scores.

- Providing test-taking strategies, such as time management and understanding the test instructions.

- Helping students identify their level of achievement and knowledge of a subject.

Drawbacks:

- Focuses attention on skills tested and neglects other important learning.

- Students focus on the outcome of a test and not on learning, which can lead to a lack of motivation and engagement.

- Instruction is affected in terms of available time.

- Test preparation does not focus on higher-level thinking skills.

Test-Taking Strategies:

- Use previous standardized tests and administer practice tests.

- Teach test format.

- Review content.

- Focus on tested skills.

- Give classroom tests that are comparable to the standardized tests.

🔧 Tools to Use

TOOL 26.1: Creating a Performance-Based Assessment from Standardized Test Questions

This tool provides steps on how to create a performance-based assessment using a standardized test question as your guide. This can help you tackle both test preparation and teaching the objectives in a meaningful way that follows best practice (Forsythe et al., 2019). The tool gives an example of how to execute the plan using a 9th grade world history example.

Step 1: Find a standardized test question. Examine various standardized tests and look for higher-level thinking questions that can more easily be adapted to a performance-based assessment.	Western civilization traditions were influenced by Emperor Constantine by A. Sending Roman soldiers to the Middle East. B. Legalizing Christianity within the Roman Empire. C. Codifying Roman law in the Middle East. D. Unifying Europe by founding the Holy Roman Empire. (Virginia Department of Education, 2014, p.14)
Step 2: Unpack the test question. Similar to selecting key terms and determining the depth of the standard, break down the question and look at the various concepts and learning that the students need to successfully answer the question.	Context: Historical thinking. Core Idea: Traditions of western civilizations were affected by different influences. Vocabulary: Codifying and legalizing. Implicit elements: Cause and effect of decisions and actions of historical figures and how they influenced people, places, and events in world history. Explicit elements: Roman Empire. Rigor: Applying social science skills to understand history. Interdisciplinary concepts: Intertwining of religion and government rule. (Forsythe et al., 2019, p.69)
Step 3: Think of links to standards and activities to incorporate into your lessons. Looking at the unpacked question, examine the standards and objectives students need to meet and determine which apply to the unpacked question. Content and level of knowledge are important.	• Apply social science skills to understand ancient Rome and its impact on Western civilization (WHI.6). • Apply social science skills to understand how Christianity developed (WHI.7). • Possible activities: create a play, create a time capsule, write a paper, give a presentation. (Virginia Department of Education, 2015, pp. 2–3)
Step 4: Create the performance assessment. Using the standards and unpacked test question, create a performance assessment that allows students to garner the same knowledge as the test question, but display their knowledge in a different manner.	Students will create a time capsule for the historical time period of 700 BCE to 500 CE. Within the time capsule, students will include different artifacts from the Roman Empire that had an implicit and explicit impact on Western civilization. These artifacts will be student-created and accompanied by a presentation explaining the significance of adding them to the time capsule. Students may work alone, in pairs, or in a small group of no more than four.
Step 5: Formulate a rubric. Create a rubric to ensure fair assessment of the performance assessment and the students' understanding of the concept and depth of knowledge.	See Chapter 27 for details on how to design a scoring rubric.

5

TOOL 26.2: Providing a Supportive Environment for Standardized Testing

In addition to the lessons you prepare for your class, it is important to be aware of how your classroom environment can impact students on a standardized test. While you may not have direct influence over these aspects, you may have flexibility in how your classroom is run during a testing time. It is also possible for you to use any classroom tests you give as an opportunity to practice creating this environment.

Timing	The time the standardized test is given impacts scores.	• First thing in the morning is the best time. After that scores decline for every hour later in the day they are given. • Giving students breaks improves average test scores. A 20–30-minute break after every hour of testing benefits all students but most especially low performing students.
Social Impacts	Students often focus on the social impacts of test taking, such as finishing first and appearing "smart" to others at the cost to their test scores. Additionally, early finishers put pressure on others to finish more quickly than they might otherwise.	• Ensure that early finishers do not leave the testing room when finished. • Encourage students to check and keep their papers until all have finished. • Prepare an individualized quiet activity to combat social pressure.

Source: Information from Phelps & Price (2016) and Sievertsen, Gino, & Piovesan (2016).

5

27 Creating or Selecting Student Rubrics that Increase Student Learning

Rubrics Enhance Student Metacognition

Words to Know

Rubric—a one- or two-page document that lays out the specific expectations for an assignment

A rubric is usually a one- or two-page document that lays out the specific expectations for an assignment. The rubric dissects an assignment into its component parts, sets forth a set of criteria for determining key learning components, and provides a detailed description of what constitutes acceptable or unacceptable levels of performance for each of those parts or criteria (Kim, 2019; Reddy & Andrade, 2010; Stevens & Levi, 2012). Rubrics usually have three major aspects:

- A coherent set of criteria,

- Descriptions of levels of performance for these criteria, and

- A scale for determining different quality levels (Brookhart, 2013; Jescovitch et al., 2019; Panadero et al., 2012).

Rubrics can be used as scoring guides for a wide variety of classroom assignments and tasks, especially those targeting complex and multidimensional performance by students. Good examples of these more complex skill or learning areas might include research papers, laboratory reports, book critiques, discussion participation, portfolios, oral presentation, and group projects (Kim, 2019; Panadero & Jönsson, 2013).

It isn't just teachers who can use rubrics to enhance learning; students who use rubrics are more knowledgeable of their learning process and learn better than students who do not (Gulzar, Buriro, & Charan, 2017; Panadero & Jönsson, 2013). For instance, when students are taught how to use a rubric to guide their writing, the quality and scores of their writing improve (Bradford et al., 2016; Greenberg, 2015; Logan & Mountain, 2018). An earlier study by Andrade (2000) found that rubrics have an exceptionally large effect size (SD = 0.99) in improving student performance in a science class, which is equivalent to a gain of 34 percentile points. Also, research finds that when rubrics are supported with exemplars, they are even more effective (Bacchus et al., 2020).

When used appropriately, rubrics are effective for

- Communicating expectations for an assignment,

- Increasing the validity and reliability of assessment,

- Facilitating teachers' ability to provide criterion-specific feedback, and

- Guiding students to monitor and evaluate their own performance (Lipnevich et al., 2014; Stronge et al., 2017).

⚒ Tools to Use

TOOL 27.1: What Makes a Rubric Effective

Rubrics improve student performance and self-reflection in many ways, especially when they demonstrate the following attributes (Bearman & Ajjawi, 2019; Greenberg, 2015; Jönsson, 2014; Jönsson & Panadero, 2017).

5

Having essential and clear criteria: A good rubric should have criteria that are aligned to important learning objectives, and it should be shared and made accessible to students early so they can use it to guide their own work. The rubric should serve as both an instructional tool as well as an evaluative one. In fact, a good rubric can help make evaluation a quality learning tool itself.

Providing transparency in assessment: You can demystify and enhance the transparency of assessment when using rubrics to convey expectations to students with clarity and explicitness and help students understand what is considered important, what to look for, and where to exert effort when learning.

- The statements of lower levels of performance should clearly describe problems that students may encounter or mistakes they may make when working on the task.

- The statements of higher levels of performance should clearly describe attributes and qualities of exemplary work that students can recognize and accomplish if they invest sufficient time and effort.

- Additionally, the gradations of ratings must be distinctive enough to allow students to identify different levels of quality.

Supporting student self-assessment: Rubrics can increase students' awareness about their own performance and serve as reference points to facilitate their planning and controlling their work in progress. Another good technique is for you to share or co-build the rubrics with students to allow the students to judge their own performance.

Providing specific feedback to students: One of the advantages of rubrics is to help you provide focused, goal-oriented feedback to students and help students to learn to use detailed feedback for improvement. Teachers can use rubrics to provide informative feedback about students' strengths and weaknesses for a given piece of work and give guidance on how to improve. The descriptions in rubrics should illustrate what lack of proficiency looks like and what mistakes students are likely to make. Additionally, rubrics should provide detailed explanations of what observable performance a student must do to demonstrate attainment of proficiency for higher levels of achievement. In essence, rubrics are far more than a grading or evaluative tool; in fact, they need not be used for formal evaluation or grading. At their best, rubrics are learning tools!

TOOL 27.2: Evaluate Your Learning Rubrics

Take out a student rubric that you have created or adopted and use the following questions to evaluate and improve the rubric.

1. How well does the rubric explicitly describe *what counts* in learning and cover all the essential attributes that define the quality of performance?
2. How is the rubric serving as both an instructional tool as well as an evaluative tool? Is it used for one or other of the purposes, or both?
3. Does the rubric cover the full scope of student performance, with the lower levels of performance clearly describing problems that students may encounter and the higher levels of performance clearly describing attributes and qualities of exemplary work that students can recognize?
4. In addition to facilitating grading, how is the rubric used to help you provide individualized, detailed, and specific feedback?
5. Through this rubric, can students gain more information about the strengths and weaknesses in their learning?
6. How is the rubric used to support students' self-regulated learning? In other words, how well does the rubric help students become more knowledgeable of their learning process through planning, monitoring, and evaluating?

5

TOOL 27.3: Design a Rubric

Now it's your turn to design or codesign with your students a rubric for an assignment and task, such as a research paper, laboratory report, book critique, Socratic seminar, portfolios, oral presentation, and group project. Consider the following steps.

1. Examine good (and bad) examples of products and identify look-fors (and red flags).
2. Cluster the look-fors into criteria. The criteria should be derived from the goals and objectives of the learning. They also should be important, understandable, and irreducible (i.e., cannot be broken down further and are distinct from each other).
3. Identify levels of performance and create clear behavior-anchored descriptions for each level. Again, the descriptions should be understandable and clearly distinguish different levels of performance.
4. Apply the rubric and revise the rubric when needed.

TOOL 27.4: Sample Rubric: Writing

Writing a rubric can seem like a big task but doing it well can give you and your students a good picture of what is expected of them in their work. This sample rubric gives you a good idea of what a comprehensive rubric looks like.

Note: Please adapt and revise the rubric based on the reading ability of your students and the criteria you truly care about and aim to measure.

Writing Rubric

Score: _____ /20

Total Score: 1–5 Unsatisfactory, 6–10 Developing/Needs Improvement, 11–15 Proficient, 16–20 Exemplary

	1: Unsatisfactory	2: Developing/Needs Improvement	3: Proficient	4: Exemplary
Ideas	• Lacks developed arguments/plot line • Has no central idea • Fails to use argumentative/narrative strategies (e.g., dialogue, character, settings, suspense, thesis statement, linking claims and evidence)	• Provides minimally developed arguments/plot line • Has weak central ideas • Attempts to use, but not effectively, argumentative/narrative strategies (e.g., dialogue, character, settings, suspense, thesis statement, linking claims and evidence)	• Provides adequately developed arguments/plot line • Has central ideas • Appropriately uses argumentative/narrative strategies (e.g., dialogue, character, settings, suspense, thesis statement, linking claims and evidence)	• Provides thoroughly developed arguments/plot line • Has strong central ideas • Highly competently uses argumentative/narrative strategies (e.g., dialogue, character, settings, suspense, thesis statement, linking claims and evidence)
Composing	• Few or no details, facts, and/or explanations • Very limited or no clear organization • Lacks a point of view: confusing structure; no transitions; many off topic ideas	• Limited details, facts, and/or explanations • Poor organization • Attempts, but lacks proficiency, in maintaining a consistent point of view; sometimes confusing structure; limited transitions; some off-topic ideas	• Adequate details, facts, and/or explanations • Logical organization, even with some minor areas for improvement • Maintains a mostly consistent point of view: mostly coherent structure: adequate transitions; most or all ideas on-topic	• Highly clear, relevant, and interesting details, facts, and/or explanations • Good organization • Maintains a consistent point of view; coherent structure; effective transitions; a strong beginning and a strong end
Word Choice/Written Expression	• General, vague, bland, repetitive word choice • Simple sentences	• Limited variety in word choice • Mostly simple sentences	• Precise and clear word choice • Many varied sentences	• Rich, interesting and creative vocabulary • Good images portrayed in work/sentence choices • Varied sentences in length and kind

5

	1: Unsatisfactory	2: Developing/Needs Improvement	3: Proficient	4: Exemplary
Voice	• Demonstrates no understanding of purpose and audience • Writer's voice cannot be heard	• Demonstrates limited understanding of purpose and audience • Writer's voice is weak	• Demonstrates appropriate understanding of purpose and audience • Effective writer's voice that creates interest in the reader	• Demonstrates clear understanding of purpose and audience • Writer's personal voice makes the writing engaging and memorable

Convention/Mechanics	• Serious flaws in use of
	  – Capitalization
	  – Punctuation
	  – Grammar
	  – Spelling
	• Errors interfere with the reader's understanding
		• Some errors in using
		  – Capitalization
		  – Punctuation
		  – Grammar
		  – Spelling
		• Errors may interfere to limited extent with the reader's understanding
			• Good use of
			  – Capitalization
			  – Punctuation
			  – Grammar
			  – Spelling
			• Few errors that do not interfere with the reader's understanding
				• Excellent use of
				  – Capitalization
				  – Punctuation
				  – Grammar
				  – Spelling
				• Very minor errors that do not interfere with the reader's understanding

5

Ensuring Assessment Improves Instruction

The Importance of Quality Assessment

As a teacher, it can feel like we are assessing students more than we are teaching them. In fact, research suggests that teachers spend as much as one-third of their classroom time in activities related to assessment (Chappuis et al., 2012). Therefore, if the information gleamed from assessment does not result in better instruction and student learning, then about 33 percent of time is wasted in the classroom. However, if the teacher is using the assessment to directly target students' instruction, then it is time well spent! There are multiple benefits when teachers monitor student progress on an ongoing and regular basis:

- Improvement in instruction;

- Decision making that reflects what is truly happening in the classroom and actual student progress;

- Better supervision of student learning, including identifying students needing different instructional modes or additional learning models and modifying teaching practices to benefit student learning; and, most importantly,

- Greater student achievement (DeLuca et al., 2016; Furtak et al., 2016; van Geel et al., 2016).

Despite the real benefits to students and teachers, it's easy to engage in a very surface level analysis of summative data by merely looking at the distribution of grades and seeing which students performed poorly and well overall. Smart teachers, instead, look more deeply at the assessment by considering how they are teaching, how students are learning, and what can be done to help individual students achieve learning objectives (Hoover & Abrams, 2013).

Words to Know

Formal assessment—a form of assessment that is data-based such as standardized tests

Informal assessment—a way of assessing students on the content and performance on a particular activity that can be variable depending on the teaching context and circumstances

Preassessment—a form of assessment that is given prior to any instruction on the concept or skills to be taught

5

The Assessment/Information Cycle

Assessing before you teach. Using assessment to inform instruction is an ongoing cycle, beginning with preassessment. While we often think of assessment occurring after instruction, preassessment allows you to determine a student's knowledge and skill *before* you teach so that you can plan for student learning needs and adapt your instruction. And it's amazing how valuable preassessment is. In fact, we've known for decades that when teachers test for prerequisite skills before they teach, student achievement increases by as much as 27 percentile points (0.7 standard deviation) (Walberg, 1984)! So, make sure you include preassessment in your repertoire of good instructional practices.

Assessing while you teach. During teaching, you should use a variety of assessments (e.g., formative, informal, summative) as part of your lessons and activities. When you intertwine assessment and instruction, the data collected can help you modify your teaching even as you teach (Mandinach, 2012). For example, if you notice during a social studies lesson that multiple students are having a hard time forming an argument for their debate, you can form a small group with those students and discuss how historians find information and form arguments. Then you can continue to monitor (i.e., collect data) these students as they work to see if your small group session helped. If the small group helped some but not others, then you analyze what works and what doesn't, and you look for a different solution on how to help the struggling students. This cycle of teaching and assessing continues as you work to meet your students' needs. In fact, formative assessment data collection may occur multiple times over the course of a unit as you tweak and adjust instruction and instructional activities to meet the students' needs.

Assessing after you teach. Finally, at the end of the unit, a summative assessment may be given to provide feedback on student learning. These data can then be used to further extend learning or reteach concepts for students moving forward. Summative assessments occur less frequently than formative assessments, but they provide information about the outcome of student learning after a period of time (Dixson & Worrell, 2016). Medical doctors use summative assessments to make importation decisions and actions, and as teachers we also need to use summative assessments to make a call about whether students are where we want them to be, how much they have mastered at the completion of a learning sequence, and whether they are ready for the next level of learning.

🔧 Tools to Use

TOOL 28.1: Flowchart for Using Assessment to Guide Instruction

This flowchart can you help you determine the steps to follow when using assessment to guide instruction.

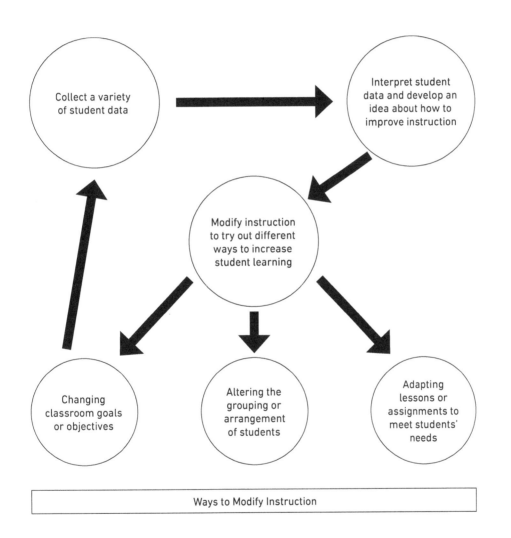

TOOL 28.2: Scenario: How to Use Summative Assessment Data to Inform Instruction

This scenario will show how you can use summative assessment data to more fully understand your students' knowledge and skills.

Mr. Murphy is a 6th grade teacher who is trying to improve his instruction by targeting students where it will make the most impact. He has collected a variety of data in different ways, including formative and summative assessments. These are the results from his students on the most recent summative assessment. In the simple chart below, he sees how students performed on the unit test, but it does not give him a clear understanding of what percentage of the material students understood, as he can only see the overall result.

Students	#Correct Out of 15	Letter Grade
Aliyah	12 (80%)	C
Kai	11 (73%)	D
Ella	13 (87%)	B
Harper	12 (80%)	C
Sasha	14 (93%)	A
Jeremy	11 (73%)	D
Arjun	12 (80%)	C
Garrett	13 (87%)	B
Emerson	12 (80%)	C
Jade	10 (67%)	D

In order to help him more clearly improve his instruction and student learning, Mr. Murphy created another chart (see below) as he graded the tests so he can see where students might have learning gaps. Based on this new information, he can create small groups for students who need more instruction on selected learning objectives and then create learning activities for student playlists (see Chapter 11) to meet individual needs.

Looking at this updated chart, he can see that Q6, Q10, and Q11 were missed by a significant number of students. This gives him feedback that something about the instruction did not resonate with his students and he needs to go back and reteach the material in a different way. In addition, he can look at these data and form a small group with Arjun, Jeremy, and Harper to go over the concept in Q9, find activities on unit objectives A for Jade, and work with Kai and Jeremy individually on their misconceptions. Having the test broken out in this way gives Mr. Murphy more useful information to plan instruction. Using the second set of data gives Mr. Murphy more information about his students. While it might take a little more time, it can help him improve his instruction and, in turn, student learning. So, the small investment in extra time pays big dividends in the long run.

Students	Sub-Unit Objectives			Sub-Unit Objectives			Sub-Unit Objectives			Sub-Unit Objectives			Sub-Unit Objectives			#Correct Out of 15	Letter Grade
	US.6.A.1	US.6.A.2	US.6.A.3	US.6.C.1	US.6.C.2	US.6.C.3	US.6.E.2	US.6.E.3	US.6.E.4	US.6.B.2	US.6.B.3	US.6.B.4	US.6.D.3	US.6.D.5	US.6.D.2		
	Q1	Q2	Q3	Q4	Q5	Q6	Q7	Q8	Q9	Q10	Q11	Q12	Q13	Q14	Q15		
Aliyah	✓	✓	✓	✓	✓			✓	✓	✓	✓		✓	✓	✓	12(80%)	C
Kai	✓	✓	✓		✓		✓	✓	✓		✓		✓	✓	✓	11(73%)	D
Ella	✓	✓	✓	✓	✓	✓	✓		✓	✓		✓	✓	✓	✓	13(87%)	B
Harper	✓	✓	✓	✓	✓	✓	✓	✓			✓	✓	✓		✓	12(80%)	C
Sasha	✓	✓	✓	✓	✓	✓	✓	✓	✓		✓	✓	✓	✓	✓	14(93%)	A
Jeremy	✓	✓		✓	✓		✓	✓			✓	✓	✓	✓	✓	11(73%)	D
Arjun	✓	✓	✓	✓	✓	✓	✓	✓		✓			✓	✓	✓	12(80%)	C
Garrett	✓	✓	✓	✓	✓	✓		✓	✓	✓		✓	✓	✓	✓	13(87%)	B
Emerson		✓	✓	✓	✓		✓	✓	✓		✓	✓	✓	✓	✓	12(80%)	C
Jade	✓			✓	✓		✓	✓	✓	✓		✓	✓	✓		10(67%)	D
# of Students with Correct Answer	9 (90%)	9 (90%)	8 (80%)	9 (90%)	10 (100%)	5 (50%)	8 (80%)	9 (90%)	7 (70%)	5 (50%)	6 (60%)	7 (70%)	10 (100%)	9 (90%)	9 (90%)		

TOOL 28.3: Data Collection Sheet

This data collection sheet allows you to place multiple forms of assessment (informal, formative, and summative) on the same page for each student. This gives you the opportunity to look closely at a student's strengths and weaknesses, as well as areas of growth, throughout the unit. This information can help you refine your instructional planning on a student-by-student basis. As you move along with the instructional unit, you can adjust your teaching and grouping of students to meet each student where they are in their understanding of the content. The boxes are broken up by standard or objective and have a space where you can jot a quick note if using a teacher observation.

To illustrate, you can see from the data sheet that Arjun had a very solid understanding of objective US.6.C. Therefore, you can arrange for him to be in a small group with other students who performed similarly on the preassessment. Likewise, you can see that even though objective US.6.B was covered on multiple occasions, there was still something Arjun was not comprehending. While the class might move on to the next unit and objectives, it will be important to go back to US.6.B and reteach differently for Arjun.

5

Student Name: Arjun **Unit:** 3		
US.6.A **1.** 3 **2.** 3 **6.** 4 **11.** 4	**US.6.B** **1.** 0 **4.** 1 **5.** 2 – in describing the concept to others had a general understanding but was confused about more specific content **6.** 2 **10.** 2 **11.** 2	**US.6.C** **1.** 3 **7.** 3 **11.** 4
US.6.D 1. 3 **3.** 4 **6.** 4 **11.** 5	**US.6.E** **1.** 1 **8.** 2 **9.** 3 **11.** 3	**Level of Understanding** Beginning = 0 Beg/Developing = 1 Developing = 2 Dev/Mastered = 3 Mastered = 4 Advanced=5

Assessment Dates and Types of Assessment

1. 11/1—Pre-Assessment on Unit 3 (formative)
2. 11/4—US.6.A—exit slip (informal)
3. 11/6—US.6.D—class work (informal)
4. 11/7—US.6.B—exit slip (formative)
5. 11/8—US.6.B—small group TO (formative)
6. 11/ 12—US.6.B/US.6.A/US.6.D—quiz (summative)
7. 11/13—US.6.C—small group work
8. 11/14—US.C.E— Three W's sheet
9. 11/15—US.C.E—Be the Teacher small group
10. 11/18—US.6.B- sticky note round up
11. 11/20—Unit Test on US.6.A-E (summative)

Source: Information adapted from The University of Chicago School Mathematics Project (2016).

5

PART 6

Finding Yourself in the Classroom

CHAPTERS 29–30

Find the joy in teaching and take care of your own well-being.

CHAPTER 29

Increasing Joy in Your Classroom

Bring Back the Joy

Emotions have always played an important part in education, whether you recognized it or not. As teachers we need to encourage the well-being of our students because their affective qualities support their academic development and skills (Norrish et al., 2013) and academic success (Suldo et al, 2011), which leads to positive school experiences. These positive school experiences, in turn, increase student happiness (Stigbaure et al., 2013), and the cycle continues.

Teachers play a powerful role in the lives of students, including older students, in terms of having the ability to promote positive emotions: happiness, joy, appreciation, engagement, hope, pride, and an array of other positive attributes. It's worth noting that joy is associated with gratitude, mindfulness, and optimism (Casioppo, 2020). It's important to note that being joyful can lead to mindfulness and being mindful can lead to joy. With the intense pressure of standards and testing in education, how can anyone feel joy? Student joy comes from the relationships built between the student and the teacher and then among other students (Baildon et al., 2019). Because of that, helping students develop and cultivate those relationships is one way to make your classroom a more joyful place.

Teachers feel joy through the positive relationships they cultivate with students (Soutter, 2020), even to the point that they often talk about "their" student(s). In particular, they experience joy in the classroom when they see student growth or have an "aha!" moment (Baildon et al., 2019). So how do we bring this state of joy for learning and just being in school to our sudents? The key is through positive relationships. Taking time to build relationships early on and continuing to cultivate them through the year, and beyond, may feel like you are taking time away from core academics, but ultimately it gives you time later in the year because students who are joyful and mindful are happier, which affects many aspects of learning. A joyful classroom is essential to the best learning classroom.

Tools to Use

TOOL 29.1: Building Relationships in the Classroom

A vital part to any classroom is building relationships because, without significant relationships, there cannot be significant learning. Positive relationships make the classroom a place where students are more satisfied, more motivated, and happier. The suggestions in this tool are just some of the ways to build relationships with students both in an individual manner and as a class.

Morning Meeting	Have a class meeting at the beginning of the day/class period and talk about non-academic topics. Example: "What is your favorite tv show and why?"
Smile	Smiling shows students that you are excited and happy to be where you are and gets them looking forward to the day/class. It's easy to forget this simple human element, so make sure you just smile!
Storytelling	Use stories to help teach your lessons for any subject and age. Stories are engaging, fun, and help make connections. Example for younger students: "My favorite number is 8 because it is shaped like a snowman, and I love snow! Well, one day the number 8 and his friend 8 ate too much snow cream and got sick on the floor. 8 and 8 got sick on the floor—8 times 8 is 64."
Student Interests	Incorporate student interests into your lesson. Example: If you know that over half the class likes the game *Among Us*, then use that knowledge to relate your lesson to the game.
Go the Extra Mile	Show students you genuinely care about them as individuals and that their education is part of who they are as a person. Reach out personally to struggling students or students who seem to be having an off day and find out how you can help.
Provide Structure	Most students respond well to having structure and knowing what is expected and when. They also appreciate fairness, so take time at the beginning of the school year to create this structure and sense of safety for students. And, of course, always practice fairness.
Have a Sense of Humor	While educating young people is important, it should also be fun. Incorporate age-appropriate and content-based humor, and you will get laughs from little ones, eye rolls from bigger ones, and a step on the positive relationship path from all.
Build Family Relationships	Communicate often with families and definitely don't wait to communicate only when things aren't going well. Communicate even to just let families know that their student had a great day! Choose a student per day and email or call home just to say how much you enjoy having them in class or relate a small positive anecdote.

Source: Information from Leskisenoja & Uusiautti (2017) and Meador (2019).

TOOL 29.2: A Joyful Room

While creating a joyful environment through building relationships with students is important for the classroom environment, the physical setting is also important because it is where learning occurs. If your classroom is dark and drab, no matter how strong your relationships are with students, joy will be stifled. The classroom is integral to the learning experience and should be warm and inviting. In fact, students report the physical environment of the classroom brings them joy (Leskisenoja & Uusiautti, 2017). This checklist will help you ensure your classroom environment is filled with joy!

- ☐ Incorporate bright colors in the classroom when possible.
- ☐ Post student work or drawings.
- ☐ Hang posters that use aphorisms or that contain uplifting messages.
- ☐ Play music at a low volume as students enter and leave the classroom.
- ☐ Make a space in your classroom that is cozy where students can go to curl up and read a good book or sit comfortably and do independent work.
- ☐ Change up the classroom setting every so often.
- ☐ Add curtains if you have windows.
- ☐ Make sure the classroom is neat and organized.
- ☐ Bring nature inside—add a plant or two to your classroom.
- ☐ Ensure all students can see themselves represented as you choose wall hangings and music.

TOOL 29.3: How to Bring More Joy into Your Classroom

There are many ways to add joy to your classroom, including through relationships, personal attributes, and engaging pedagogical practices. This tool is a set of ideas to add joy to the classroom and make school a place where both you and the students want to be! While not always easy to incorporate, working to add one of these aspects to the day may transform the school experience for you and your students.

6

Teach with Joy	• Be excited about your subject, your lessons, and your job; your enthusiasm and joy will be contagious.
Show Interest	• Show interest in your students' lives outside the classroom. • Show interest in their learning. • Take 30 seconds to 1 minute with individuals when they first enter the room and talk to them. Rotate which students you meet with daily.
Make Assessment Meaningful	• Assessment is important and students will put forth more effort and find more joy from an assessment that has meaning to them. • An example would be a performance assessment or portfolio piece.
Build Classroom Community	• Ensure that student ideas, understandings, and viewpoints are valued and shared. • Taking 5 minutes at the beginning of class to have a class meeting will help build community. Use buddy activities.
Authentic Intellectual Work	• Higher level thinking can be challenging; unfortunately, some students may get frustrated and give up if the work does not feel authentic to them. • An example might be to have science students create an experiment using the items provided to them.
Variety	• Use a variety of teaching strategies. It is boring to you and the students if lessons are monotonous and the same. • Provide opportunities for experiential learning, such as fieldtrips or fieldwork. • Incorporate the arts, which will prompt imagination and creativity. • Use games to teach or reinforce content.
Student Autonomy	• Students have joy in learning when they are given the opportunity to be the leaders of their own learning. • An example may have students choosing or creating their own projects to complete instead of being told which to complete.
Connect Students to Subject Matter	• Connect students to the subject matter in a way that makes it meaningful to them. • An example would be using the musical *Hamilton* to engage students in American history. Have them create their own musical from the topic you are teaching. • Use something in the students' everyday experience to connect new material to prior knowledge. • An example could be to use memes to help make new information memorable.
Allow Students to See Themselves in the Content	• Joy comes from a sense of belonging, and a way to help students feel they belong is to make sure they can identify with the content on a personal level. • Make sure students are reflected in the materials in the classroom and in the content being taught. • Invite families into the classroom to give presentations on topics at which they excel.

Source: Information from Baildon et al. (2019) and Lekisenoja & Uusiautti (2017).

30 Taking Care of Your Own Well-Being

Why the Need for Self-Care?

Teachers help mold the minds of the future and therefore have a vital role in our society. Sadly, many teachers from countries all around the world suffer from "chronic, work-related stress, which negatively affects their health, life satisfaction, vocation, and professional stability" (Gustems-Carnicer & Calderon, 2019, p.1). In fact, the percentage of teachers in the United States who are affected by stress has increased from 30 percent to 46 percent (Gustems-Carnicer & Calderon, 2019), which is nearly half of all teachers! This personal strain contributes to far too many new teachers leaving the profession within the first five years of teaching (Gallant & Riley, 2017). Due to this staggering stress-related picture, it is important for new teachers to be satisfied in their careers and, importantly, know how to manage the stress and feel empowered.

Job Satisfaction

The health and well-being of teachers not only affects the teachers themselves but also students and the educational system as a whole. Teachers who are satisfied in their job have higher student achievement (Dicke et al., 2019). Therefore, job satisfaction is an important predictor when looking at teacher retention and turnover as well as student achievement, motivation, and disciplinary climate (Dicke et al., 2019). Looking more carefully at teacher work, it's important to note that multiple factors play a role in teacher job satisfaction, including such diverse issues as working conditions, school climate, staff collegiality, career and administrative support, school leadership, practices related to diverse student populations, and decision making (Dicke et al., 2019; Crisci et al., 2019). These issues are important predictors in job satisfaction. In addition to all these external factors, teachers themselves tend to feel more personally satisfied in their jobs when they have personal achievement, recognition, responsibility, interpersonal relationships, self-efficacy, and autonomy (Crisci et al., 2019).

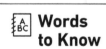

Words to Know

Teacher self-efficacy—a teacher's belief that their work plays an important role in students' learning and development

How to Improve Job Satisfaction

With all this information you probably wonder how you can positively influence your job satisfaction. One way is to build relationships with colleagues in your building as well as the administration. Building these relationships helps

- Improve the climate of the school,

- Provide you with a sense of collegiality (even if you are the new teacher on the block),

- Facilitate closer ties with administration and provide administrative support, and

- Facilitate interpersonal relationships that help you become more satisfied within your job.

In addition to building these important relationships within your school community, it is important to take care of your own health. While personal factors as noted above give personal job satisfaction, they are not directly associated with well-being (Jeon et al., 2018). Therefore, it is vital for you to find ways to care for your well-being outside of your job, and it's fair to say that healthy and happy teachers make better teachers.

Words to Know

Mindfulness—the state of being in which you are conscious or aware of your thoughts or actions

How to Take Care of Yourself

Across the profession, teachers tend to be seen as selfless, giving their time and attention to the academic and social well-being of the students in their class. Nonetheless, teachers need to understand that too much of a good thing can be detrimental to their health. Due to the many demands the teaching profession places on teachers, it is easy to become overwhelmed, stressed, or even depressed. One way you can defeat these harmful feelings is to examine your own beliefs. For instance, teachers who feel they are competent in their craft feel less stress and depression; however, they still may feel emotionally exhausted (Jeon et al., 2018). If you ever start to question your competence as a teacher, use the support system you have built to improve your job satisfaction. Another way to improve your health is to participate in mindfulness activities. It is important to know when you are feeling stressed and how to take steps to lessen that feeling so you can prevent burnout. Participating in a teacher support program can help you identify signs of stress and use techniques (e.g., simple breathing techniques) to help lower harmful and negative feelings (Schussler et al., 2016; Beshai et al., 2016). We don't intend to advocate for a single way to address stress and its related complications; rather, we simply want to remind you that it is important for you to take care of yourself for your own health, for your career, and for the students you work with on a daily basis.

🔧 Tools to Use

TOOL 30.1: Protecting Teachers Against Stress

This self-assessment chart gives you an overview of three traits that help protect teachers from too much stress: increasing empathy, character strengths, and coping strategies. The chart is meant to help you recognize where you find yourself psychologically and help you protect yourself from undue stress. If you recognize yourself using a coping strategy linked to distress, try using a different one.

Words to Know

Character strengths—dispositions that people possess that enable well-being

Coping strategies—actions or thoughts that allow a person to make adjustments in stressful situations

Empathy—an affective response that allows a person to understand where others are emotionally

	Never	Rarely	Sometimes	Often	Always
Increase Empathy Having empathy helps teachers recognize the needs of others, especially their students, which in turn leads to their ability to support and provide for individual needs.					
I have successful relationships with others that make me happy.					
I am well liked by others and have a community of support.					
I interact with others in a positive way and can put myself in others' shoes.					
Strength of Character Building and maintaining strong and healthy relationships benefits feelings of well-being and helps teachers focus on others.					
I work well with a team and am a good team member.					
I trust others and am trustworthy.					
I know how to build and maintain strong and healthy relationships.					
I have a sense of humor and do not take things too seriously.					
I am honest with myself and others.					
I have a sense of wonder and am curious about how things work or how they came to be.					
I am persistent and do not give up easily, even when things are challenging.					

6

	Never	Rarely	Sometimes	Often	Always
Coping Strategies Having strategies to help relieve stress and anxiety helps benefit feelings of accomplishment and well-being.					
When faced with a problem, I look at it from a logical point of view as opposed to an emotional point of view.					
When difficulties come, I try to keep a positive stance and try to evaluate the situation from a positive position as opposed to having a negative mindset.					
When I become overwhelmed, I reach out to those around me for love, support, and a listening ear.					
When I feel challenged, I use problem-solving techniques to try and reframe the problem.					
Signs of Distress Signs of distress may be affecting your well-being. If you recognize these signs in yourself, reach out to others for help and try using a more positive coping strategy.					
I avoid situations and people or put off tasks that are challenging or difficult.					
When I feel challenged, I tend to use problem-solving techniques that do not help or are from an emotional point of view as opposed to a logical point of view.					

Source: Information from Gustems-Carnicer & Calderon (2019).

TOOL 30.2: Personal Mindfulness Routine

The steps in this tool are a way for you to start creating your own personal mindfulness routine (Pal et al., 2018). These steps can be done daily to help focus your mind on what is going on around you. In stressful moments in the classroom, it is OK to take a moment to recalibrate and practice mindfulness. In addition to the primary benefits, it also shows your students how you take care of yourself.

1. Sit in a relaxed position.
2. Take three to five long, deep breaths.
3. Focus on a small goal for the day, either just for yourself or in relationship to others (e.g., I will be patient with myself, I will pause and think before I speak, I will be patient with my students, I will ask for help when needed).
4. During the day, check in with your progress toward your daily goal.
5. If need be, during the day, stop what you are doing, take a few deep breaths, and do a reset or refocus.

TOOL 30.3: How to Block Burnout

Teacher burnout is a function of the cognitive and emotional demands placed on the profession of teaching. As a teacher, it is important to recognize that you have to take care of yourself and take steps to ensure the time spent working in the teaching profession isn't wasted by burning out. This tool gives you three categories where you can make changes to help prevent burnout. Making a change in one area will influence the others and help you de-stress.

Awareness	Steps to Increase Awareness:	Awareness Activities:
	1. Keep "green" thoughts and toss "red" thoughts: Green thoughts are positive thoughts and self-talk; red thoughts are negative thoughts or self-talk. 2. Be mindful: Pay attention to the small things around you and the impact they have in the world.	1. Be mindful of your thoughts. When you catch yourself having a "red" thought, let go of it and replace it with a "green" thought. 2. Let go of things that cause you to have a negative mindset or cause you to have "red" thoughts. 3. Meditate with an app or on your own. 4. Use yoga or pilates for movement with mindfulness. 5. Be present—let go of the past and do not worry about the future.
Attitude	Steps to Change Attitude:	Attitude Activities:
	1. Gratitude: Show appreciation for small things. 2. "This too shall pass": Recognize that this moment is finite and will end. 3. Optimism: Recognize that adversity is temporary. 4. Empathy: Feel the same emotions as others in a similar manner. 5. Forgiveness: Consciously let go of anger, regret, resentment, disappointment, or vengeance.	1. Every day think about 1–2 things for which you are grateful. After a week or two increase this to 5 things a day. 2. Pause a moment to take a few deep breaths, and recognize that "this too shall pass" and that where you are now is not where you will always be. 3. Forgive yourself. Recognize what you need to improve upon and then let go of it. 4. Empathize with others and make a positive connection. 5. Embrace your vulnerability. It is OK to ask questions or to ask for help from colleagues.
Action	Steps to Change Your Actions:	Action Activities:
	1. Self-determination: Determine the who, what, why, and when of your teaching. Take control over how your teaching practice is nurtured. 2. Self-sacrifice: Promote someone else's welfare without increasing your own. 3. Goal setting: Create goals for yourself both inside and outside teaching.	1. Perform random acts of kindness. 2. Set healthy boundaries in your life with respect to your job as well as with people. 3. Create goals—both short-term and long-term. 4. Have deeper, more connected conversations with colleagues. 5. Build a positive tribe of supports both in school and outside of school. 6. Determine the type of teacher you want to be. Take professional development classes that help you with that goal. 7. Examine your to-do list and then trim your list and focus your attention to those that work toward your goals.

Source: Adapted from Mielke (2019).

Acknowledgments

We want to begin by acknowledging the many wonderful teachers from whom we learned on our own educational pathways. Your devotion and deep knowledge, your masterfulness in delivering quality teaching and engaging us, and your ability to inspire us to be better people is beyond our ability to fully describe. While we won't attempt to name each of you, know that we remember the lessons you taught us about teaching—and about living better lives. The model you epitomized, to a large degree, inspired us to become teachers.

In addition, we extend special thanks to two of our colleagues at Stronge & Associates Educational Consulting: Dr. Lauri Leeper, Director of Instructional Design and Development, and Dr. Virginia Tonneson, Chief Operating Officer. Lauri helped frame the ideas for this book, and her input and thoughts are reflected in many of the tools. Additionally, early preparatory conversations with her shaped the topics and scope of the chapters. Ginny contributed in so many ways to this and every project we undertake. Her steady, insightful guidance and engagement helped make the book a reality. Ginny and Lauri, we express our deepest gratitude to you!

Finally, we wish to acknowledge Genny Ostertag, Managing Director of Book Acquisitions & Editing for ASCD, for her confidence in our work and for her support throughout the book development process. Additionally, we sincerely appreciate the careful and thoughtful guidance that Megan Doyle, ASCD editor, provided throughout the important processes of editing and proofing the manuscript. It is the capable and conscientious professionals that have made publishing with ASCD a pleasure. Thank you!

References

Adler, D. A. (2016) *Prices! Prices! Prices!: Why they go up and down*. Holiday House.

Aelterman, N., Vansteenkiste, M., & Haerens, L. (2019). Correlates of students' internalization and defiance of classroom rules: A self-determination theory perspective. *British Journal of Educational Psychology, 89*(1), 22–40.

Akhlaq, M., Chudhary, M. A., Malik, S., ul-Hassan, S., Mehmood, K. (2010). An experimental study to assess the motivational techniques used by teachers in the teaching of chemistry. *Journal of Education and Sociology, 3,* 36–52.

Alotaibi, N. R. (2017). Overview on preparing teachers to understand twice-exceptional students. *International Interdisciplinary Journal of Education, 6*(3), 359–370.

Alter, P., & Haydon, T. (2017). Characteristics of effective classroom rules: A review of the literature. *Teacher Education and Special Education, 40*(2), 114–127.

Anderson, D. M., McGuire, F. A., & Cory, L. (2011). The first day: It happens only once. *Teaching in Higher Education, 16*(3), 293–303.

Anderson, L. W., & Krathwohl, D. R. (Eds.). (2001). *A taxonomy for learning, teaching, and assessing: A revision of Bloom's taxonomy of educational objectives* (Complete ed.). Longman.

Andrade, H. G. (2000). Using rubrics to promote thinking and learning. *Educational Leadership, 57*(5), 13–18.

Bacchus, R., Colvin, E., Knight, E. B., & Ritter, L. (2020). When rubrics aren't enough: Exploring exemplars and student rubric co-construction. *Journal of Curriculum & Pedagogy, 17*(1), 48–61.

Baildon, M., Chelva Rajah S. N., & Suhaimi Afandi. (2019). Sparking joy in history classrooms. *HSSE Online, 8*(1), 66–76.

Baker, K. (n.d). *Questions to ask when you're at a new school*. Teaching Made Practical. https://teachingmadepractical.com/questions-new-school/

Baliram, N., & Ellis, A. K. (2019). The impact of metacognitive practice and teacher feedback on academic achievement in mathematics. *School Science & Mathematics, 119*(2), 94–104.

Banes, L. C., Ambrose, R. C., Bayley, R., Restani, R. M., & Martin, H. A. (2018). Mathematical classroom discussion as an equitable practice: Effects on elementary English learners' performance. *Journal of Language, Identity & Education, 17*(6), 416–433.

Bang, H. (2012). Promising homework practices: Teachers' perspectives on making homework work for newcomer immigrant students. *The High School Journal, 95,* 3–31. doi:10.1353/hsj.2012.0001

Barak, M. (2017). Science teacher education in the twenty-first century: A pedagogical framework for technology-integrated social constructivism. *Research in Science Education, 47*(2), 283–303.

Barrett, P., Davies, F., Zhang, Y., & Barrett, L. (2015). The impact of classroom design on pupil's learning: Final results of a holistic, multi-level analysis. *Building and Environment, 89,* 113–133.

Barrett, P., Davies, F., Zhang, Y., & Barrett, L. (2017). The holistic impact of classroom spaces on learning in specific subjects. *Environment and Behavior, 49*(4), 425–451.

Bearman, M., & Ajjawi, R. (2019). Can a rubric do more than be transparent? Invitation as a new metaphor for assessment criteria. *Studies in Higher Education*. DOI: 10.1080/03075079.2019.1637842.

Bembenutty, H. (2011). The first word: Homework's theory, research, and practice. *Journal of Advanced Academics, 22*(2), 185–193. https://doi.org/10.1177/1932202X1102200201

Bernacki, M. L., Greene, J. A., & Crompton, H. (2020). Mobile technology, learning, and achievement: Advances in understanding and measuring the role of mobile technology in education. *Contemporary Educational Psychology, 60,* https://doi.org/10.1016/j.cedpsych.2019.101827

Beshai, S., McAlpine, L., Weare, K., & Kuyken, W. (2016). A non-randomized feasibility trial assessing the efficacy of a mindfulness-based intervention for teachers to reduce stress and improve well-being. *Mindfulness, 7*(1), 198–208.

Bickel, T. (2020). *Where do I sit* [Unpublished master's thesis]. California State University San Marcos.

Borich, G. D. (2006). *Effective teaching methods.* Pearson Prentice Hall.

Bradford, K. L., Newland, A. C., Rule, A. C., & Montgomery, S. E. (2016). Rubrics as a tool in writing instruction: Effects on the opinion essays of first and second graders. *Early Childhood Education Journal, 44*(5), 463–472.

Brame, C. (2013). Writing good multiple choice test questions. https://cft.vanderbilt.edu/guides-sub-pages/writing-good-multiple-choice-test-questions/

Breen, A. (2019, October 7). *Renowned educator and scholar Carol Tomlinson defined a new way of teaching.* UVA Today. https://news.virginia.edu/content/renowned-educator-and-scholar-carol-tomlinson-defined-new-way-teaching

Bressman, S., Winter, J. S., & Efron, S. E. (2018). Next generation mentoring: Supporting teachers beyond induction. *Teaching and Teacher Education, 82,* 162–170.

Brookhart, S. M. (2013). *How to create and use rubrics for formative assessment and grading.* ASCD.

Brown, C. (2018). What motivated A-level students to achieve? Exploring the role of expectations and task values. *Psychology of Education Review, 42*(1), 53–63.

California Department of Education. (2000). History-social science content standards for California public schools: Kindergarten through grade twelve. https://www.cde.ca.gov/ci/hs/cf/

Callahan, R. M. (2013). The English learner dropout dilemma: Multiple risks and multiple resources. California Drop out Research Project.

Campbell, K. H. (2018). Back-to-school night: The focus could be love. *Northwest Journal of Teacher Education, 13*(1), 1–10. https://doi.org/10.15760/nwjte.2018.13.1.7

Carrasco, D., & Irribarra, D. T. (2018). The role of classroom discussion. In A. Sandoval-Hernández, M. Isac, D. Miranda (Eds). *Teaching Tolerance in a Globalized World. IEA Research for Education* (pp. 87–101). Springer, Cham.

Casey, A., & Fernandez-Rio, J. (2019). Cooperative learning and the affective domain. *Journal of Physical Education, Recreation & Dance, 90*(3), 12–17.

Casioppo, D. (2020). The cultivation of joy: Practices from the Buddhist tradition, positive psychology, and yogic philosophy. *The Journal of Positive Psychology, 15*(1), 67–73.

Center for Disease Control and Prevention. (n.d.). *Preventing bullying.* https://www.cdc.gov/violenceprevention/youthviolence/bullyingresearch/fastfact.html

Chaaban, Y., & Du, X. (2017). Novice teachers' job satisfaction and coping strategies: Overcoming contextual challenges at Qatari government schools. *Teaching and Teacher Education, 67,* 340–350.

Chambers, D., Jones, P., & Riley, M. W. (2017). Belonging and the relationship to whole schooling: Introduction to themed issue. *International Journal of Whole Schooling, 13*(1), 1–5.

Chappuis, J., Stiggins, R. J., Chappuis, S., & Arter, J. A. (2012). *Classroom assessment for student learning: Doing it right-using it well* (2nd ed.). Pearson.

Christofferson, M., & Sullivan, A. L. (2015). Preservice teachers' classroom management training: A survey of self-reported training experiences, content coverage, and preparedness. *Psychology in the Schools, 52*(3), 248–264.

Clay, B. (2001). Is this a trick question: A short guide to writing effective test questions. https://www.k-state.edu/ksde/alp/resources/Handout-Module6.pdf

Conrad, J. (1990). *Heart of darkness.* Dover Publications.

Cook, C. R., Fiat, A., Larson, M., Daikos, C., Slemrod, T., Holland, E. A., Thayer, A. J., & Renshaw, T. (2018). Positive greetings at the door: Evaluation of a low-cost, high-yield proactive classroom management strategy. *Journal of Positive Behavior Interventions, 20*(3), 149–159.

Cooper, H. (1989a). *Homework.* Longman.

Cooper, H. (1989b). Synthesis of research on homework. *Educational Leadership, 47*(3), 85–91.

Council of Chief State School Officers. (2013, April). Interstate teacher assessment and support consortium InTASC model core teaching standards and learning progressions for teachers 1.0: A resource for ongoing teacher development. Author.

Crisci, A., Sepe, E., & Malafronte, P. (2019). What influences teachers' job satisfaction and how to improve, develop and reorganize the school activities associated with them. *Quality & Quantity, 53*(5), 2403–2419.

Curtis, D. A., & Moore, K. (2018). The first day of class: Starting with an activity or syllabus? *North American Journal of Psychology, 20*(3).

Danielson, M., Strom, B., & Kramer, K. (2011). Real homework tasks: A pilot study of types, values, and resource requirements. *Educational Research Quarterly, 35*(1), 17–32.

David-Ferdon, C., Vivolo-Kantor, A. M., Dahlberg, L. L., Marshall, K. J., Rainford, N., & Hall, J. E. (2016). *A comprehensive technical package for the prevention of youth violence and associated risk behaviors.* National Center for Injury Prevention and Control, Centers for Disease Control and Prevention.

Dean, C. B., & Hubbell, E. R., Pitler, H., & Stone, B. (2012). *Classroom instruction that works: Research-based strategies for increasing student achievement.* ASCD.

De Arment, S. T., Reed, E., & Wetzel, A. P. (2013). Promoting adaptive expertise: A conceptual framework for special educator preparation. *Teacher Education and Special Education*, 36, 217–230.

DeLuca, C., LaPointe-McEwan, D., & Luhanga, U. (2016). Teacher assessment literacy: A review of international standards and measures. *Educational Assessment, Evaluation, and Accountability, 28*, 251–272.

Dennie, D., Acharya, P., Greer, D., & Bryant, C. (2019). The impact of teacher–student relationships and classroom engagement on student growth percentiles of 7th and 8th grade students. *Psychology in the Schools, 56*(5), 765–780.

Dettmers, S., Trautwein, U., Lüdtke, O., Kunter, M., & Baumert, J. (2010). Homework works if homework quality is high: Using multilevel modeling to predict the development of achievement in mathematics. *Journal of Educational Psychology, 102*(2), 467.

Dicke, T., Marsh, H. W., Parker, P. D., Guo, J., Riley, P., & Waldeyer, J. (2019). Job satisfaction of teachers and their principals in relation to climate and student achievement. *Journal of Educational Psychology.* https://www.emerald.com/insight/content/doi/10.1108/IJEM-04-2014-0057/full/html

DiDonato-Barnes, N., Fives, H., & Krause, E. S. (2014). Using a table of specifications to improve teacher-constructed traditional tests: An experimental design. *Assessment in Education: Principles, Policy & Practice, 21*(1), 90–108.

Dietiker, L., Males, L. M., Amador, J. M., & Earnest, D. (2018). Research commentary: Curricular noticing: A framework to describe teachers' interactions with curriculum materials. *Journal for Research in Mathematics Education, 49*(5), 521–532.

Dimitroff, A., & Dimitroff, A. (2018). New beginnings: Trials and triumphs of newly hired teachers. *Eurasian Journal of Applied Linguistics, 4*(2), 135–153. DOI: 10.32601/ejal.464090

Dixson, D. D., & Worrell, F. C. (2016). Formative and summative assessment in the classroom. *Theory Into Practice, 55,* 153–159.

D'Mello, S. (2012). Monitoring affective trajectories during complex learning. *Encyclopedia of the Sciences of Learning* (pp. 2325–2328). Springer.

Dolezal, S. E., Welsh, L. M., Pressley, M., & Vincent, M. M. (2003). How third-grade teachers motivate student academic achievement. *The Elementary School Journal, 103,* 239–267.

Durlak, J. A., Weissberg, R. P., Dymnicki, A. B., Taylor, R. D., & Schellinger, K. B. (2011). The impact of enhancing students' social and emotional learning: A meta-analysis of school-based universal interventions. *Child Development, 82*(1), 405–432.

Dymnicki, A., Sambolt, M., & Kidron, Y. (2013). Improving college and career readiness by incorporating social and emotional learning. *College and Career Readiness and Success Center.*

Engin, G. (2020). An examination of primary school students' academic achievement and motivation in terms of parents' attitudes, teacher motivation, teacher self-efficacy and leadership approach. *International Journal of Progressive Education, 16*(1), 257–276.

Ertel, P. K. (2020). Five key strategies for conducting effective parent–teacher conferences. In A. M. Quinzio-Zafran & E. A. Wilkins (Eds.), *The new teacher's guide to overcoming common challenges: Curated advice from award-winning teachers* (pp. 163–164). Routledge.

Erturan-Ilker, G. (2014). Effects of feedback on achievement goals and perceived motivational climate in physical education. *Issues in Educational Research, 24*(2), 152–161.

Eskine, K. E., & Hammer, E. Y. (2017). Students' perspectives on the first day of class: A replication. *International Journal for the Scholarship of Teaching and Learning, 11*(1), n1.

Fan, H., Xu, J., Cai, Z., He, J., & Fan, X. (2017). Homework and students' achievement in math and science: A 30-year meta-analysis, 1986–2015. *Educational Research Review, 20,* 35–54. DOI: 10.1016/j.edurev.2016.11.003

Fenton, P., Ocasio-Stoutenburg, L., & Harry, B. (2017). The power of parent engagement: Sociocultural considerations in the quest for equity. *Theory Into Practice, 56*(3), 214–225.

Ferrara, M. M. (2017). Understanding family engagement through the focus of the national standards for family-school partnerships: Secondary preservice teachers' perspectives. *School Community Journal, 27(2),* 145–166.

Finley, T. (2015, December 15). 22 powerful closure activities. *Edutopia.* https://www.edutopia.org/blog/22-powerful-closure-activities-todd-finley

Fisher, D., Frey, N., & Almarode, J. (2020a). Student learning communities as builders of collective efficacy. *Reading Psychology, 41*(6), 559–582.

Fisher, D., Frey, N., & Almarode, J. (2020b). *Student learning communities: A springboard for academic and social-emotional development.* ASCD.

Fitzmaurice, H., Flynn, M., & Hanafin, J. (2020). Primary teachers' homework practices: Identity, expectations, policies and cultural values. *Issues in Educational Research, 30*(3), 897–919.

Flores, O. J., & Kyere, E. (2020). Advancing equity-based school leadership: The importance of family–school relationships. *The Urban Review,* 1–18.

Ford, D. Y. (2005). Welcoming all students to room 202: Creating culturally responsive classrooms. *Gifted Child Today, 28*(4), 28–65.

Forsythe, M., Jackson, J., & King, J. (2019). Turning tests into tasks. *Science Scope, 42*(7), 67–74.

Francis, E. M. (2016). *Now that's a good question! How to promote cognitive rigor through classroom questions.* ASCD.

Frenzel, A. C., Taxer, J. L., Schwab, C., & Kuhbandner, C. (2019). Independent and joint effects of teacher enthusiasm and motivation on student motivation and experiences: A field experiment. *Motivation and Emotion, 43,* 255–265.

Furtak, E. M., Kiemer, K., Circi, R. K., Swanson, R., deLeon, V., Morrison, D., & Heredia, S. C. (2016). Teachers' formative assessment abilities and their relationship to student learning: Findings from a four-year intervention study. *Instructional Science, 44,* 267–291.

Gaikhorst, L., Beishuizen, J., Roosenboom, B., & Volman, M. (2017). The challenges of beginning teachers in urban primary schools. *European Journal of Teacher Education, 40*(1), 46–61. DOI:10.1080/02619768.2016.1251900.

Gallant, A., & Riley, P. (2017). Early career teacher attrition in Australia: Inconvenient truths about new public management. *Teachers and Teaching: Theory and Practice, 23,* 896–913. http://dx.doi.org/10.1080/13540602.2017.1358707

Gallup. (2018). *Gallup student poll: Engaged today—ready for tomorrow.* https://www.gallup.com/education/233537/gallup-student-poll.aspx

García-Carmona, M., Marín, M. D., & Aguayo, R. (2019). Burnout syndrome in secondary school teachers: A systematic review and meta-analysis. *Social Psychology of Education, 22,* 189–208.

Gareis, C. R., & Grant, L. W. (2015). *Teacher-made assessments: How to connect curriculum, instruction, & student learning* (2nd ed.). Eye on Education.

Garvey, W., O'Connor, M., Quach, J., & Goldfeld, S. (2020). Better support for children with additional health and developmental needs in school settings: Perspectives of education experts. *Childcare, Health and Development, 46*(4), 522–529.

Gebril, A., & Eid, M. (2017). Test preparation beliefs and practices in a high-stakes context: A teacher's perspective. *Language Assessment Quarterly, 14*(4), 360–379.

Gillies, R. M. (2016). Dialogic interactions in the cooperative classroom. *International Journal of Educational Research, 76,* 178–189.

Gillies, R. M. (2019). Promoting academically productive student dialogue during collaborative learning. *International Journal of Educational Research, 97,* 200–209.

Gladden, R. M., Vivolo-Kantor, A. M., Hamburger, M. E., & Lumpkin, C. D. (2014). *Bullying surveillance among youths: Uniform definitions for public health and recommended data elements, version 1.0.* National Center for Injury Prevention and Control, Centers for Disease Control and Prevention and U.S. Department of Education.

Göçmençelebi, Ş. İ., Özkan, M., & Bayram, N. (2012). Evaluating primary school students' deep learning approach to science lessons. *International Online Journal of Educational Sciences, 4*(3), 554–562.

Gottfried, M. A., & Ansari, A. (2019). Raising the bar: Teaching kindergarteners with emotional and behavioral disabilities and teachers' readiness expectations. *Early Childhood Research Quarterly, 48,* 75–83.

Green, G. P., Bean, J. C., & Peterson, D. J. (2013). Deep learning in intermediate microeconomics: Using scaffolding assignments to teach theory and promote transfer. *Journal of Economic Education, 44*(2), 142–157.

Green, Z. A., & Batool, S. (2017). Emotionalized learning experiences: Tapping into the affective domain. Evaluation and program planning, 62, 35–48.

Greenberg, K. P. (2015). Rubric use in formative assessment: A detailed behavioral rubric helps students improve their scientific writing skills. *Teaching of Psychology, 42*(3), 211–217.

Greene, J. A., Copeland, D. Z., Deekens, V. M., & Seung, B. Y. (2018). Beyond knowledge: Examining digital literacy's role in the acquisition of understanding in science. *Computers & Education, 117,* 141–159.

Gremmen, M. C., van den Berg, Y. H., Segers, E., & Cillessen, A. H. (2016). Considerations for classroom seating arrangements and the role of teacher characteristics and beliefs. *Social Psychology of Education, 19*(4), 749–774.

Guler, N. (2020). Preparing to teach English language learners: Effect of online courses in changing mainstream teachers' perceptions of English language learners. *Innovation in Language Learning and Teaching, 14*(1), 83–96. DOI:10.1080/17501229.2018.1494736

Gulzar, M. A., Buriro, G. A., & Charan, A. A. (2017). Investigating the effects of rubrics on assessment of writing tasks. *International Research Journal of Arts and Humanities, 45,* 191–206.

Guo, W., & Wei, J. (2019). Teacher feedback and students' self-regulated learning in mathematics: A study of Chinese secondary students. *Asia-Pacific Education Researcher, 28*(3), 265–275.

Gustems-Carnicer, J., & Calderon, C. (2019). Well-being and the preparation of teachers. In *Oxford Research Encyclopedia of Education.* https://oxfordre.com/education/view/10.1093/acrefore/9780190264093.001.0001/acrefore-9780190264093-e-757

Hale, M. S., & City, E. A. (2006). *The teacher's guide to leading student-centered discussions: Talking about texts in the classroom.* Corwin.

Hamilton, L. (2019). Banish the graveyard: How does classroom layout affect students' engagement? In G. Geng, P. Smith, P. Black, Y. Budd, and L. Disney (Eds.), *Reflective Practice in Teaching* (pp. 21–25). Springer.

Hampden-Thompson, G., & Galindo, C. (2016). School-family relationships, school satisfaction and the academic achievement of young people. *Educational Review, 69*(2), 248–265. DOI: 10.1080/00131911.2016.1207613

Hargreaves, A. (2019). Teacher collaboration: 30 years of research on its nature, forms, limitations and effects. *Teachers and Teaching 25*(5), 603–621. DOI: 10.1080/13540602.2019.1639499

Hartell, E., & Strimel, G. J. (2018). What is it called and how does it work: Examining content validity and item design of teacher-made tests. *International Journal of Technology and Design Education 29*(1), 781–802. https://doi.org/10.1007/s10798-018-9463-2

Harwin, A. (2019, November 25). Twice exceptional students miss out on gifted classes. *Education Week.* https://www.edweek.org/teaching-learning/twice-exceptional-students-miss-out-on-gifted-classes/2019/11

Hattie, J. (2009). *Visible learning: A synthesis of over 800 meta-analyses relating to achievement.* Routledge.

Hattie, J. (2012). *Visible learning for teachers: Maximizing impact on learning.* Routledge.

Hattie, J. (2017a, November). *250+ influences on student achievement.* Visible Learning Plus. https://visible-learning.org/wp-content/uploads/2018/03/VLPLUS-252-Influences-Hattie-ranking-DEC-2017.pdf

Hattie, J. (2017b). *Hattie ranking: 252 influences and effect sizes related to student achievement.* Visible Learning. https://visible-learning.org/hattie-ranking-influences-effect-sizes-learning-achievement/

Hattie, J. A. C., & Timperley, H. (2007). The power of feedback. *Review of Educational Research, 77*(1), 81–112.

Hayes, L. (2020). Developing routines and minimizing disruption. In E. Overland, J. Barber, and M. Sackvlle-Ford. (Eds.). *Classroom management: An essential guide for student and newly qualified teachers* (pp. 22–34). Routledge.

Herrmann, Z. (2019). Cooperate or collaborate? *Educational Leadership 76*(1), 68–72.

Holte, K. L. (2016). Homework in primary school: Could it be made more child-friendly? *Studia Paedagogica,* 21(4), 13–33. https://doi.org/10.5817/SP2016-4-1

Hoover, N. R., & Abrams, L. M. (2013). Teachers' instructional use of summative student assessment data. *Applied Measurement in Education, 26(3),* 219–231.

Hudson, P. (2013). Forming the mentor-mentee relationship. *Journal of Mentoring and Tutoring* 24(1), 30–43.

Ingersoll, R. M., & Strong, M. (2011). The impact of induction and mentoring programs for beginning teachers: A critical review of the research. *Review of educational research, 81*(2), 201–233.

Ismail, E. A., & Groccia, J. E. (2018). Students engaged in learning. *New Directions for Teaching & Learning, 154,* 45–54.

Isoldi, R. (2021). Personal correspondence.

Izadinia, M. (2016). Student teachers' and mentor teachers' perceptions and expectations of a mentoring relationship: Do they match or clash? *Professional Development in Education, 42*(3), 387–402.

Jeasik, C. H. O., James, J., & Swarts, G. (2020). The impact of US pre-service teachers' high-stakes, accountability era schooling experiences on their future teaching practices. *Journal of Teacher Education and Educators, 9*(2), 143–167.

Jeon, L., Buettner, C. K., & Grant, A. A. (2018). Early childhood teachers' psychological well-being: Exploring potential predictors of depression, stress, and emotional exhaustion. *Early Education and Development, 29*(1), 53–69.

Jescovitch, L. N., Scott, E. E., Cerchiara, J. A., Doherty, J. H., Wenderoth, M. P., Merrill, J. E., Urban-Lurain, M., & Haudek, K. C. (2019). Deconstruction of holistic rubrics into analytic rubrics for large-scale assessments of students' reasoning of complex science concepts. *Practical Assessment, Research & Evaluation, 24*(7), 1–13.

Jeynes, W. (2012). A meta-analysis of the efficacy of different types of parental involvement programs for urban students. *Urban Education, 47*(4), 706–742.

Jeynes, W. H. (2018). A practical model for school leaders to encourage parental involvement and parental engagement. *School Leadership and Management, 38*(2), 147–163.

Johnsen, S. K. (2017). How to differentiate in today's schools. *Gifted Child Today, 40*(3), 129.

Johnson, A. P. (2019, March 15). *The hunter lesson plan format and other teaching recipes.* LinkedIn. https://www.linkedin.com/pulse/hunter-lesson-plan-format-other-teaching-recipes-andrew-johnson/

Jokikokko, K., Uitto, M., Deketelaere, A., & Estola, E. (2017). A beginning teacher in emotionally intensive micropolitical situations. *International Journal of Educational Research, 81*(1), 61–70. Elsevier Ltd. https://www.learntechlib.org/p/203281/

Jönsson, A. (2014). Rubrics as a way of providing transparency in assessment. *Assessment & Evaluation in Higher Education, 39*(7), 840–852.

Jönsson, A., & Panadero, E. (2017). The use and design of rubrics to support assessment for learning. In D. Carless, S. Bridges, C. Chan, and R. Glofcheski. (Eds). *Scaling up assessment for learning in higher education: The enabling power of assessment* (pp. 99–111). Springer.

Josephson, J., Wolfgang, C., & Mehrenberg, R. (2018, June). Strategies for supporting students who are twice-exceptional. *Journal of Special Education Apprenticeship, 7*(2).

Kane, R. G., & Francis, A. (2013). Preparing teachers for professional learning: Is there a future for teacher education in new teacher induction? *Teacher Development, 17*(3), 362–379.

Kanno, Y., & Cromley, J. G. (2013). English language learners' access to and attainment in postsecondary education. *Tesol Quarterly, 47*(1), 89–121.

Kaur, M. (2017). To recognize, realize and differentiate the learning needs of students. *Pertanika Journal of Social Sciences & Humanities, 25*(2), 503–510.

Kearney, S. (2017). Beginning teacher induction in secondary schools: A best practice case study. *Issues in Educational Research, 27*(4), 784–802.

Kim, J. (2019). Effects of rubric-referenced self-assessment training on Korean high school students' English writing. *English Teaching, 74*(3), 79–111.

Kinay, İ., & Ardiç, T. (2017). Investigating teacher candidates' beliefs about standardized testing. *Universal Journal of Educational Research, 5*(12), 2286–2293.

Konold, T., Cornell, D., Jia, Y., & Malone, M. (2018). School climate, student engagement, and academic achievement: A multilevel multi-informant examination. *AERA Open.* https://doi.org/10.1177/2332858418815661

Kraft, M. A. (2017). Engaging parents as partners in education through better communication. *Educational Leadership, 75*(1), 58–62.

Kraft, M. A., & Dougherty, S. M. (2013). The effect of teacher-family communication on student engagement: Evidence from a randomized field experiment. *Journal of Research on Educational Effectiveness, 6*(3), 199–222.

Krathwohl, D. R., Bloom, B. S., & Masia, B. B. (1964). Taxonomy of educational objectives: The classification of educational goals. Handbook II: Affective domain. Longman.

Larson, K. E., Pas, E. T., Bradshaw, C. P., Rosenberg, M. S., & Day-Vines, N. L. (2018). Examining how proactive management and culturally responsive teaching relate to student behavior: Implications for measurement and practice. *School Psychology Review, 47*(2), 153–166.

Lee, C. W., & Ritchotte, J. A. (2018, January). Seeing and supporting twice-exceptional learners. *The Educational Forum 82*(1), 68–84.

Lee, O. (2018). English language proficiency standards aligned with content standards. *Educational Researcher, 47*(5), 317–327.

Lei, H., Cui, Y., & Zhou, W. (2018). Relationships between student engagement and academic achievement: A meta-analysis. *Social Behavior and Personality: An International Journal, 46*(3), 517–528.

Leskisenoja, E., & Uusiautti, S. (2017). How to increase joy at school? Findings from a positive-psychological intervention at a Northern-Finnish school. *Education in the North, 24*(2), 36–55.

Lester, R. R., Allanson, P. B., & Notar, C. E. (2017). Routines are the foundation of classroom management. *Education, 137*(4), 398–412.

Lipnevich, A. A., McCallen, L. N., Miles, K. P., & Smith, J. K. (2014). Mind the gap! Students' use of exemplars and detailed rubrics as formative assessment. *Instructional Science, 42,* 539–559.

Lim, W., Son, J., & Kim, D. (2016). Understanding preservice teacher skills to construct lesson plans. *International Journal of Science and Math Education, 16,* 519–538. http://doi.org/10.1007/s10763-016-9783-1

Lin, C. (2019). Effective classroom management in drama English class. *Advances in Social Science, Education and Humanities Research, 378,* 134–139.

Liu, R., Ye, L., & Guo, M. (2016, July). Research on the influence of mentoring relationship on improving the career satisfaction of young teachers in universities and colleges—The moderating effect of gender. In 2016 International Conference on Logistics, Informatics and Service Sciences (LISS) (pp. 1–5). IEEE.

Logan, K., & Mountain, L. (2018). Writing instruction in chemistry classes: Developing prompts and rubrics. *Journal of Chemical Education, 95*(10), 1692–1700.

Mahoney, M. (2020, January). Implementing evidence-based practices within multi-tiered systems of support to promote inclusive secondary classroom settings. *Journal of Special Education Apprenticeship, 9*(1).

Malinen, O., & Savolainen, H. (2016). The effect of perceived school climate and teacher efficacy in behavior management on job satisfaction and burnout: A longitudinal study. *Teaching and Teacher Education, 60,* 144–152.

Malinowsky, L. R. (2020). Planning for successful parent-teacher conferences: A navigation guide. In A. M. Quinzio-Zafram & E. A. Wilkins (Eds.), *The new teacher's guide to overcoming common challenges* (pp. 207–210). Routledge.

Mandinach, E. B. (2012). A perfect time for data use: Using data-driven decision making to inform practice. *Educational Psychologist, 47*(2), 71–85.

Marzano, R. J., Pickering, D. J., & Pollock, J. E. (2001). *Classroom instruction that works: Research-based strategies for increasing student achievement.* ASCD.

McCoach, D. B., Siegle, D., & Rubenstein, L. D. (2020). Pay attention to inattention: Exploring ADHD symptoms in a sample of underachieving gifted students. *Gifted Child Quarterly, 64*(2), 100–116.

McKee, R. J. (2015). Encouraging classroom discussion. *JSSE-Journal of Social Science Education, 66*–73.

McKnight, K., O'Malley, K., Ruzic, R., Horsley, M. K., Franey, J. J., & Bassett, K. (2016). Teaching in a digital age: How educators use technology to improve student learning. *Journal of research on technology in education, 48*(3), 194–211.

McLean, A. (2003). *The motivated school.* Sage.

McLean, L., Sparapani, N., Connor, C. M., & Day, S. (2020). Students' problem behaviors and teachers' warmth and demand as predictors of students' classroom instructional experiences in first grade. *Contemporary Educational Psychology, 61.* https://doi.org/10.1016/j.cedpsych.2020.101863

McLean, L., Sparapani, N., Toste, J. R., & Connor, C. M. (2016). Classroom quality as a predictor of first graders' time in non-instructional activities and literacy achievement. *Journal of School Psychology, 56,* 45–58.

Meador, D. (2019, July 5). Strategies for teachers to develop positive relationships with students. ThoughtCo. https://www.thoughtco.com/develop-positive-relationships-with-students-3194339

Mielke, C. (2019). *The burnout cure: Learning to love teaching again.* ASCD.

Molbaek, M. (2018). Inclusive teaching strategies—Dimensions and agendas. *International Journal of Inclusive Education, 22*(10), 1048–1061.

Murphy, P. K., Wilkinson, I. A. G., Soter, A. O., Hennessey, M. N., & Alexander, J. F. (2009). Examining the effects of classroom discussion on students' comprehension of text: A meta-analysis. *Journal of Educational Psychology, 101*(3), 740–764.

Nagro, S. A., Fraser, D. W., & Hooks, S. D. (2019). Lesson planning with engagement in mind: Proactive classroom management strategies for curriculum instruction. *Intervention in School and Clinic, 54*(3), 131–140.

National Association for Gifted Children. (n.d.). What is giftedness? http://www.nagc.org/resources-publications/resources/what-giftedness

National Center for Education Statistics. (2021). English language learners in public schools. *Condition of Education.* U.S. Department of Education, Institute of Education Sciences. https://nces.ed.gov/programs/coe/indicator/cgf

National Institute of Justice (NIJ), US Department of Justice, Office of Justice Programs, & United States of America. (2020, November 13). Anti-bullying intervention for teachers shows positive, short-term outcomes. https://nij.ojp.gov/topics/articles/anti-bullying-intervention-teachers-shows-positive-short-term-outcomes

Ngeow, K., & Kong, Y.-S. (2003). *Learning through discussion: Designing tasks for critical inquiry and reflective learning.* ERIC Clearinghouse on Reading English and Communication.

Nguyen, D., & Ng, D. (2020). Teacher collaboration for change: Sharing, improving, and spreading. *Professional Development in Education 46*(4), 638–651. DOI: 10.1080/19415257.2020.1787206

Nolet, V., & McLaughlin, M. J. (2005). *Accessing the general curriculum: Including students with disabilities in standards-based reform* (2nd ed.). Corwin.

Norazman, N., Ismail, A. H., Ja'afar, N. H., Khoiry, M. A., & Ani, A. I. C. (2019). A review of seating arrangements towards the 21st century classroom approach in schools. *Malaysian Journal of Sustainable Environment, 6*(2), 21–46.

Norrish, J. M., Williams, P., O'Connor, M., & Robinson, J. (2013). An applied framework for positive education. *International Journal of Well-Being, 3*(2), 147–161.

North Carolina Association of Educators. (2020, June 19). 30 questions to ask during the first days of school: Make your life easier by learning school procedures early on. National Education Association. https://www.nea.org/professional-excellence/student-engagement/tools-tips/30-questions-ask-during-first-days-school

Ocak, G., & Karafil, B. (2020). Development of teacher feedback use evaluation scale. *International Journal of Progressive Education, 16*(1), 287–299.

Olweus, D. (1993). *Bullying at school.* Blackwell Publishing.

Orlich, D. C., Harder, R. J., Callahan, R. C., Trevisan, M. S., & Brown, A. H. (2012). *Teaching strategies: A guide to effective instruction* (9th ed.). Cengage Learning.

Pal, P., Hauck, C., Goldstein, E., Bobinet, K., & Bradley, C. (2018). 5 simple mindfulness practices for daily life. Mindful. https://www.mindful.org/take-a-mindful-moment-5-simple-practices-for-daily-life/

Panadero, E., & Jönsson, A. (2013). The use of scoring rubrics for formative assessment purposes revisited: A review. *Educational Research Review, 9,* 129–144.

Panadero, E., Tapia, J. A., & Huertas, J. A. (2012). Rubrics and self-assessment scripts effects on self-regulation, learning, self-efficacy in secondary education. *Learning and Individual Differences, 22,* 806–813.

Pas, E. T., Waasdorp, T. E., & Bradshaw, C. P. (2019). Coaching teachers to detect, prevent, and respond to bullying using mixed reality simulation: An efficacy study in middle schools. *International Journal of Bullying Prevention, 1*(1), 58–69.

PEBC. (2016, September 19). *Mentors! 6 tips for connecting with new teachers.* Public Education and Business Coalition. https://www.pebc.org/mentors-6-tips-for-connecting-with-new-teachers/

Phelps, C., & Price, J. (2016). Slowing the hare: Quick finishers and class performance on standardized tests. *Learning and Individual Differences, 51,* 322–326.

Pillet-Shore, D. M. (2016). Criticizing another's child: How teachers evaluate students during parent-teacher conferences. *Language in Society, 45*(1), 33–58.

Pollock, J. E. (2007). *Improving student learning: One teacher at a time.* ASCD.

Porter, C. (2018). *Planning to co-teach with ELL teachers: How discourse positions teachers within professional learning communities* [Doctoral dissertation, The University of Iowa].

Puentedura, R. R. (2013). SAMR: Moving from enhancement to transformation [Portable Document Format Slides]. http://www.hippasus.com/rrpweblog/archives/2013/05/29/SAMREnhancementToTransformation.pdf

Quaigrain, K., & Arhin, A. K. (2017). Using reliability and item analysis to evaluate a teacher-developed test in educational measurement and evaluation. *Cogent Education 4*(1). https://doi.org/10.1080/2331186X.2017.1301013

Reddy, Y. M., & Andrade, H. (2010). A review of rubric use in higher education. *Assessment and Evaluation in Higher Education, 35*(4), 435–448.

Reese, T. (2014). Lesson closure: Stick the landing. *Education Update, 56*(6), 5.

Reyes, M. R., Brackett, M. A., Rivers, S. E., White, M., & Slovey, P. (2012). Classroom emotional climate, student engagement, and academic achievement. *Journal of Educational Psychology, 104*(3), 700–712.

Richmond, W. K. (2018). *The school curriculum*. Routledge.

Rigby, K. (2020). How teachers deal with cases of bullying at school: What victims say. *International Journal of Environmental Research and Public Health, 17*(1), 2338–2349.

Rodrigues, P. F. S., & Pandeirada, J. N. S. (2018). When visual stimulation of surrounding environment affects children's cognitive performance. *Journal of Experimental Child Psychology, 176*, 140–149.

Rogers, K. B. (2007). Lessons learned about educating the gifted and talented: A synthesis of the research on educational practice. *Gifted Child Quarterly, 51*(4), 382–396.

Ronfeldt, M., & McQueen, K. (2017). Does new teacher induction really improve retention? *Journal of Teacher Education, 68*(4), 394–410.

Rosário, P., Núñez, J. C., Vallejo, G., Cunha, J., Nunes, T., Mourão, R., & Pinto, R. (2015). Does homework design matter? The role of homework's purpose in student mathematics achievement. *Contemporary Educational Psychology, 43*, 10–24.

Rosário, P., Núñez, J. C., Vallejo, G., Nunes, T., Cunha, J., Fuentes, S., & Valle, A. (2018). Homework purposes, homework behaviors, and academic achievement: Examining the mediating role of students' perceived homework quality. *Contemporary Educational Psychology*. https://doi.org/10.1016/j.cedpsych.2018.04.001

Saarento, S., Boulton, A. J., & Salmivalli, C. (2015). Reducing bullying and victimization: Student-and classroom-level mechanisms of change. *Journal of Abnormal Child Psychology, 43*(1), 61–76.

Sambiase, M. (2021). Personal correspondence.

Scales, P. C., Boekel, M. V., Pekel, K., Syvertsen, A. K., & Roehlkepartain, E. C. (2020). Effects of developmental relationships with teachers on middle-school students' motivation and performance. *Psychology in the Schools, 57*(4), 646–677. https://doi.org/10.1002/pits.22350

Schmidt, J. A., Kafkas, S. S., Maier, K. S., Shumow, L., & Kackar-Cam, H. Z. (2019). Why are we learning this? Using mixed methods to understand teachers' relevance statements and how they shape middle school students' perceptions of science utility. *Contemporary Educational Psychology, 57*, 9–31.

School Specialty. (2018, October 1). 5 ways to make your classroom a bully-free zone. https://blog.schoolspecialty.com/5-ways-make-classroom-bully-free-zone/

Schuetz, R. L., Biancarosa, G., & Goode, J. (2018). Is technology the answer? Investigating students' engagement in math. *Journal of Research on Technology in Education, 50*(4), 318–332.

Schussler, D. L., Jennings, P. A., Sharp, J. E., & Frank, J. L. (2016). Improving teacher awareness and well-being through CARE: A qualitative analysis of the underlying mechanisms. *Mindfulness, 7*(1), 130–142.

Senko, C., & Harackiewicz, J. (2005). Regulation of achievement goals: The role of competency feedback. *Journal of Educational Psychology, 97*(3), 320–336.

Sentse, M., Veenstra, R., Kiuru, N., & Salmivalli, C. (2015). A longitudinal multilevel study of individual characteristics and classroom norms in explaining bullying behaviors. *Journal of Abnormal Child Psychology, 43*(5), 943–955.

Shelton, S. A., & Brooks, T. (2019). "We need to get these scores up": A narrative examination of the challenges of teaching literature in the age of standardized testing. *Journal of Language and Literacy Education, 15*(2), 1–17.

Sievertsen, H. H., Gino, F., & Piovesan, M. (2016). Cognitive fatigue influences students' performance on standardized tests. *Proceedings of the National Academy of Sciences, 113*(10), 2621–2624.

Sklad, M., Diekstra, R., Ritter, M. D., Ben, J., & Gravesteijn, C. (2012). Effectiveness of school based universal social, emotional, and behavioral programs: Do they enhance students' development in the area of skill, behavior, and adjustment? *Psychology in the Schools, 49*, 892–909.

Smets, W. (2017). High quality differentiated instruction—A checklist for teacher professional development on handling differences in the general education classroom. *Universal Journal of Educational Research, 5*(11), 2074–2080.

Smith, T. E., & Sheridan, S. M. (2019). The effects of teacher training on teachers' family-engagement practices, attitudes, and knowledge: A meta-analysis. *Journal of Educational and Psychological Consultation, 29*(2), 128–157. https://doi.org/10.1080/10474412.2018.1460725

Smith-Adcock, S., Swank, J., Greenidge, T., & Henesy, R. (2019). Standing up or standing by? Middle school students and teachers respond to bullying: A responsive program evaluation. *Counseling Outcome Research and Evaluation, 10*(1), 49–62.

Soland, J., & Sandilos, L. E. (2021). English language learners, self-efficacy, and the achievement gap: Understanding the relationship between academic and social-emotional growth. *Journal of Education for Students Placed at Risk (JESPAR), 26*(1), 20–44.

Sousa, D. A. (2011). *How the brain learns* (4th ed.). Corwin.

Soutter, M. (2020). Measuring joy: A social justice issue. *Phi Delta Kappan, 101*(8), 25–30.

Spoden, C., & Fricke, K. (2018). Measurement of teachers' reactive, preventive and proactive classroom management skills by student ratings—Results from a two-level confirmatory factor analysis. *Psychological Test and Assessment Modeling, 60*(2), 223–240.

St-Amand, J., Girard, S., & Smith, J. (2017). Sense of belonging at school: Defining attributes, determinants, and sustaining strategies. *IAFOR Journal of Education, 5*(2), 105–119.

Stevens, D. D., & Levi, A. J. (2012). *Introduction to rubrics: An assessment tool to save grading time, convey effective feedback and promote student learning* (2nd ed.). Stylus Publishing.

Stigbaure, B., Gnambs, T., Gamsjäger, M., & Batinic, B. (2013). The upward spiral of adolescents' positive school experiences and happiness: Investigating reciprocal effects over time. *Journal of School Psychology, 51*(2), 231–242.

Stronge & Associates. (2018). *How to create high-quality assessments.* ASCD.

Stronge, J. H. (2018). *Qualities of effective teachers* (2nd ed.). ASCD.

Stronge, J. H., Grant, L. W., & Xu, X. (2017). *Designing effective assessments.* Solution Tree.

Stronge, J. H., & Xu, X. (2016). *Instructional planning for effective teaching.* Solution Tree.

Suldo, S. M., Thalji, A., & Ferron, J., (2011). Longitudinal academic outcomes predicted by early adolescents' subjective well-being, psychopathology, and mental health status yielded from a dual factor model. *Journal of Positive Psychology, 6*(1), 17–30.

Sun, R. C., & Shek, D. T. (2012). Student classroom misbehavior: An exploratory study based on teachers' perceptions. *The Scientific World Journal.* https://doi.org/10.1100/2012/208907

Suprayogi, M. N., Valcke, M., & Godwin, R. (2017). Teachers and their implementation of differentiated instruction in the classroom. *Teaching and Teacher Education, 67*, 291–301.

Süral, S., & Dedebali, N. C. (2018). A study of curriculum literacy and information literacy levels of teacher candidates in department of social sciences education. *European Journal of Educational Research, 7*(2), 303–317.

Taylor, E. S., & Tyler, J. H. (2012). Can teacher evaluation improve teaching. *Education Next, 12*(4), 78–84.

Taylor, R. D., Oberle, E., Durlak, J. A., & Weissberg, R. P. (2017). Promoting positive youth development through school-based social and emotional learning interventions: A meta-analysis of follow-up effects. *Child Development, 88*(4), 1156–1171.

Teo, P. (2019). Teaching for the 21st century: A case for dialogic pedagogy. *Learning, Culture and Social Interaction, 21*, 170–178.

TESOL International Association. (2006). *PreK–12 English language proficiency standards.* Author.

Thornberg, R., Wänström, L., & Jungert, T. (2018). Authoritative classroom climate and its relations to bullying victimization and bystander behaviors. *School Psychology International, 39*(6), 663–680.

Tobia, V., Sacchi, S., Cerina, V., Manca, S., & Fornara, F. (2020). The influence of classroom seating arrangement on children's cognitive processes in primary school: The role of individual variables. *Current Psychology,* 1–12.

Tomlinson, C. A. (2014). *The differentiated classroom: Responding to the needs of all learners* (2nd ed.). ASCD.

Tomlinson, C. A. (2015). Teaching for excellence in academically diverse classrooms. *Society, 52*(3), 203–209.

Tomlinson, C. A. (2017). Differentiated instruction. In C. M. Callahan & H. L. Hertberg-Davis (Eds.), *Fundamentals of gifted education: Considering multiple perspectives* (2nd ed.) (pp. 287–300). Routledge.

Tóth-Pjeczka, K., Papos, N., Szivák, J. (2019). Components, models and operational mechanisms of teacher collaboration. In M. Kowalczuk-Walêdziak, A. Korzeniecka-Bondar, W. Danilewicz, and G. Lauwers

(Eds.), *Rethinking teacher education for the 21st century: Trends, challenges and new directions* (pp 283–299). Verlag Barbara Budrich.

Trautwein, U., Niggli, A., Schnyder, I., & Lüdke, O. (2009). Between-teacher differences in homework assignments and the development of students' homework effort, homework emotions, and achievement. *Journal of Educational Psychology, 101*(1), 176–189. DOI:10.1037/0022-0663.101.1.176.

Tze, V. M. C., Daniels, L. M., & Klassen, R. M. (2016). Evaluating the relationship between boredom and academic outcomes: A meta-analysis. *Educational Psychology Review, 28*(1), 119–144.

U.S. Department of Education. (2015). *Every student succeeds act.* Author. https://www.gpo.gov/fdsys/pkg/BILLS-114s1177enr/pdf/BILLS-114s1177enr.pdf

United States Government. (n.d.). *Understanding the roles of early education and child care providers in community-wide bullying prevention efforts.* Stopbullying.gov. https://www.stopbullying.gov/sites/default/files/2017-09/hrsa_guide_early-education-child-care-providers_508v2.pdf

The University of Chicago School Mathematics Project. (2016). *Everyday mathematics assessment handbook.* McGraw Hill.

van Geel, M., Keuning, T., Frèrejean, J., Dolmans, D., van Merriënboer, J., & Visscher, A. J. (2019). Capturing the complexity of differentiated instruction. *School Effectiveness and School Improvement, 30*(1), 51–67.

van Geel, M., Keuning, T., Visscher, A. J., & Fox, J. (2016). Assessing the effects of a school-wide data-based decision-making intervention on student achievement growth in primary schools. *American Educational Research Journal, 53*(2),360–394.

Vangrieken, K., Dochy, F., Raes, E., & Kyndt, E. (2015). Teacher collaboration: A systematic review. *Educational Research Review, 15,* 17–40.

Vangrieken, K., Meredith, C., Packer, T., & Kyndt, E. (2017). Teacher communities as a context for professional development: A systematic review. *Teaching and Teacher Education, 61,* 47–59.

Vatterott, C. (2018). *Rethinking homework: Best practices that support diverse needs.* ASCD.

Virginia Department of Education. (2014). *Virginia standards of learning test item set world history I 2008 history and social science standards of learning.* https://www.doe.virginia.gov/testing/sol/released_tests/index.shtml

Virginia Department of Education. (2015). *History and social standards of learning for Virginia public schools for world history and geography to 1500 A.D. (C.E.).* https://www.doe.virginia.gov/testing/sol/standards_docs/history_socialscience/index.shtml

Vygotsky, L. S. (1978). *Mind in society: The development of higher mental processes.* Harvard University Press.

Wachs, S., Bilz, L., Niproschke, S., & Schubarth, W. (2019). Bullying intervention in schools: A multilevel analysis of teachers' success in handling bullying from the students' perspective. *The Journal of Early Adolescence, 39*(5), 642–668.

Walberg, H. J. (1984). Improving the productivity of America's schools. *Educational Leadership, 41*(8), 19–27.

Walsh, J. A., & Sattes, B. D. (2015). *Questioning for classroom discussion: Purposeful speaking, engaged listening, deep thinking.* ASCD.

Wassermann, S. (2010). Effective classroom discussions. *Educational Leadership, 67*(5). http://www.ascd.org/publications/educational-leadership/feb10/vol67/num05/Effective-Classroom-Discussions.aspx

Waters, S., & Mashburn, N. (2017). An investigation of middle school teachers' perceptions on bullying. *Journal of Social Studies Education Research, 8*(1), 1–34.

Waterworth, P. (2020). Creating joyful learning within a democratic classroom. *Journal of Teaching and Learning in Elementary Education, 3*(2), 109–116.

Webb, N. (1997). *Research monograph number 6: Criteria for alignment of expectations and assessments on mathematics and science education.* CCSSO.

Weimer, K. R. (2018). Maximizing mentoring relationships. *General Music Today, 32*(2), 12–17.

Weinberg, A. (2021, September 23). Solid foundation mentoring relationship. *Edutopia.* https://www.edutopia.org/article/solid-foundation-mentoring-relationship/

Weiss, H. B., Kreider, H., Lopez, M. E., & Chatman-Nelson, C. M. (2014). *Preparing educators to engage families: Case studies using an ecological framework.* Sage.

Weyer, M. (2018, May). Understanding and assisting English language learners in school. National Conference of State Legislatures. https://www.ncsl.org/research/education/understanding-and-assisting-english-language-learners-in-school.aspx

Wigelsworth, M., Lendrum, A., Oldfield, J., Scott, A., Ten Bokkel, I., Tate, K., & Emery, C. (2016). The impact of trial stage, developer involvement and international transferability on universal social and emotional learning programme outcomes: A meta-analysis. *Cambridge Journal of Education, 46*(3), 347–376.

Wiggins, G. (2012). Seven keys to effective feedback. *Educational Leadership, 70*(1), 10–16.

Wiley, K. R. (2020). The social and emotional world of gifted students: Moving beyond the label. *Psychology in the Schools, 57*(10), 1528–1541.

Xu, X. (2020, March 5). How to provide effective verbal feedback in the classroom. *The International Educator.* https://www.tieonline.com/article/2678/how-to-provide-effective-verbal-feedback-in-the-classroom

Yeager, D. S., Purdie-Vaughns, V., Garcia, J., Apfel, N., Brzustoski, P., et al. (2014). Breaking the cycle of mistrust: Wise interventions to provide critical feedback across the racial divide. *Journal of Experimental Psychology: General, 143*(2), 804–824.

Yuan, R., Zhang, J., & Yu, S. (2018). Understanding teacher collaboration processes from a complexity theory perspective: A case study of a Chinese secondary school. *Teachers and Teaching 24(5),* 520–537. DOI: 10.1080/13540602.2018.1447458

Zhu, Y., & Leung, F. (2012). Homework and mathematics achievement in Hong Kong: Evidence from the TIMSS 2003. *International Journal of Science and Mathematics Education, 10*(4), 907–925.

Zimmaro, D. M. (2016). Writing good multiple-choice exams. University of Texas–Austin. https://facultyinnovate.utexas.edu/sites/default/files/writing-good-multiple-choice-exams-fic-120116.pdf

Index

The letter *f* following a page locator denotes a figure.

About the Authors

James H. Stronge is President and CEO of Stronge & Associates Educational Consulting, LLC, an educational consulting company that focuses on teacher and leader effectiveness with projects throughout the United States and internationally. Additionally, he is the Heritage Professor of Education, a distinguished professorship, in the Educational Policy, Planning, and Leadership Area at the College of William and Mary, in Williamsburg, Virginia. He teaches doctoral courses within the School of Education's Educational Policy, Planning, and Leadership (EPPL) Program, with a particular focus on teacher and leader effectiveness, human resource leadership, legal issues in education, and research design.

Dr. Stronge's research interests include policy and practice related to teacher quality and effectiveness, teacher and administrator evaluation, and teacher selection. He has worked with numerous state departments of education, school districts, and national and international educational organizations to design and implement evaluation and hiring systems for teachers, administrators, and support personnel. Recently, he completed work on new teacher and principal evaluation systems for American international schools in conjunction with the Association of American Schools in South America and supported by the U.S. Department of State. Stronge has made more than 350 presentations at regional, national, and international conferences and conducted workshops for educational organizations extensively throughout the United States and internationally. Among his current research projects are 1) international comparative studies of national award-winning teachers in the United States and China, and 2) influences of economic and societal trends on student academic performance in countries globally. His most recent books include *What Makes a World-Class School and How We Can Get There* (2017, ASCD), *Qualities of Effective Teachers, 3rd Edition* (2018, ASCD), *Qualities of Effective Principals, 2nd Edition* (2021, ASCD), and *International Beliefs and Practices that Characterize Teacher Effectiveness* (co-editor) (2021, IGI Global).

Stronge has authored, coauthored, or edited 34 books and more than 200 articles, chapters, and technical reports. He was a founding member of the board of directors for the Consortium for Research on Educational Assessment and Teacher Effectiveness, and he was selected as the 2012 national recipient of the Millman Award from CREATE in recognition of his work in the field of teacher and administrator evaluation.

Jessica Straessle received her master's degree in Early Childhood Education from Georgia State University, where she focused on effective teaching in an urban environment. She then received her Doctor of Philosophy degree from William and Mary's Educational Policy, Planning, and Leadership Program with a focus on curriculum and educational leadership. While completing her PhD program, she was a classroom teacher teaching inclusion and gifted classes. Currently, she is working as a research associate with Stronge & Associates Educational Consulting. Her research interests include teacher effectiveness, teacher evaluation, and student individuality. To date, she has helped edit two books and coauthored three quick reference guides for teachers (ASCD).

Xianxuan Xu received her Doctor of Philosophy degree from William and Mary's Educational Policy, Planning, and Leadership Program. Currently she is working as the Decision Analytics Researcher at the Virginia Department of Education. Previously she served as the Senior Research Associate with Stronge & Associates. Her research interests include teacher and principal effectiveness, professional development, and evaluation. She also is interested in conducting international comparative studies on educational effectiveness. To date, she has authored or coauthored eight books and numerous book chapters, journal articles, and technical reports. She has presented findings of her research at leading national conferences, such as the American Educational Research Association, the University Council for Educational Administration, and the CREATE National Evaluation Institute.

Related Resources

At the time of publication, the following resources were available (ASCD stock numbers in parentheses).

The Classroom Behavior Manual: How to Build Relationships with Students, Share Control, and Teach Positive Behaviors by Scott Ervin (#122033)

High-Quality Lesson Planning (Quick Reference Guide) by Jane E. Pollock (#QRG118050)

How to Align Assessment to Curriculum and Instruction (Quick Reference Guide) by James H. Stronge (#QRS118086)

How to Create High-Quality Assessments: Qualities of Effective Teaching (Quick Reference Guide) by James H. Stronge (#QRS118085)

How to Give Effective Feedback to Your Students, 2nd Edition by Susan M. Brookhart (#116066)

How to Use Assessments to Inform Instruction (Quick Reference Guide) by James H. Stronge (#QRS118087)

The New Classroom Instruction That Works: The Best Research-Based Strategies for Increasing Student Achievement by Bryan Goodwin and Kristin Rouleau (#122032)

Qualities of Effective Teachers, 3rd Edition by James H. Stronge (#118042)

For up-to-date information about ASCD resources, go to www.ascd.org. You can search the complete archives of *Educational Leadership* at www.ascd.org/el. To contact us, send an email to member@ascd.org or call 1-800-933-2723 or 703-578-9600.